Virgil *Aeneid* VIII

The following titles are available from Bloomsbury for the OCR specifications in Latin and Greek, first teaching September 2016

Cicero *Pro Milone*: A Selection, with introduction by Lynn Fotheringham and commentary notes and vocabulary by Robert West

Ovid *Heroides*: A Selection, with introduction, commentary notes and vocabulary by John Godwin

Propertius, Tibullus and Ovid: A Selection of Love Poetry, with introduction, commentary notes and vocabulary by Anita Nikkanen

Seneca Letters: A Selection, with introduction, commentary notes and vocabulary by Eliot Maunder

Tacitus *Annals* I: A Selection, with introduction by Roland Mayer and commentary notes and vocabulary by Katharine Radice

Virgil *Aeneid* VIII: A Selection, with introduction, commentary notes and vocabulary by Keith Maclennan

Virgil *Aeneid* X: A Selection, with introduction, commentary notes and vocabulary by Christopher Tanfield

OCR Anthology for Classical Greek GCSE, covering the prescribed texts by Homer, Herodotus, Euripides, Lucian, Plato and Plutarch, edited by Judith Affleck and Clive Letchford

OCR Anthology for Classical Greek AS and A-level, covering the prescribed texts by Aristophanes, Homer, Plato, Sophocles, Thucydides and Xenophon, with introduction, commentary notes and vocabulary by Malcolm Campbell, Rob Colborn, Frederica Daniele, Ben Gravell, Sarah Harden, Steven Kennedy, Matthew McCullagh, Charlie Paterson, John Taylor and Claire Webster

Supplementary resources for these volumes can be found at www.bloomsbury.com/OCR-editions
Please type the URL into your web browser and follow the instructions to access the Companion Website. If you experience any problems, please contact Bloomsbury at academicwebsite@bloomsbury.com

Virgil *Aeneid* VIII:
A Selection

Lines 86–279, 558–84

With introduction, commentary notes and
vocabulary by Keith Maclennan

Bloomsbury Academic
An imprint of Bloomsbury Publishing Plc

B L O O M S B U R Y
LONDON · OXFORD · NEW YORK · NEW DELHI · SYDNEY

Bloomsbury Academic

An imprint of Bloomsbury Publishing Plc

50 Bedford Square	1385 Broadway
London	New York
WC1B 3DP	NY 10018
UK	USA

www.bloomsbury.com

BLOOMSBURY and the Diana logo are trademarks of Bloomsbury Publishing Plc

First published 2016

Introduction, commentary notes and vocabulary © Keith Maclennan, 2016

Keith Maclennan has asserted his right under the Copyright, Designs and Patents Act, 1988, to be identified as Editor of this work.

British Library Cataloguing-in-Publication Data

A catalogue record for this book is available from the British Library.

ISBN:	PB:	978-1-47427-190-5
	ePub:	978-1-47427-192-9
	ePDF:	978-1-47427-193-6

Library of Congress Cataloging-in-Publication Data

A catalog record for this book is available from the Library of Congress.

Typeset by RefineCatch Limited, Bungay, Suffolk

Printed and bound in Great Britain

Contents

Preface

The text and notes found in this volume are designed to guide any student who has mastered Latin up to GCSE level and wishes to read Virgil's work in the original.

The edition is, however, particularly designed to support students who are reading *Aeneid* VIII in preparation for OCR's AS Latin examination June 2017–June 2018. (Please note this edition uses AS to refer indiscriminately to AS and the expected first year of A Level, i.e. Group 1.) The *Aeneid* as a whole is worth reading for the brilliance, variety and intensity of Virgil's narrative, and important for its central place in the literature of the Roman Empire and of modern Europe. In the lines covered here Aeneas, the forefather of Rome, visits the site of the city four hundred years before it is founded and hears a story of Hercules and how he helped make the place habitable for Aeneas' successors.

This edition contains a detailed introduction to the historical and literary context of the Aeneid with a detailed explanation of the metre and its use. The notes to the text itself aim to help students bridge the gap between GCSE and AS Level Latin; points of linguistic difficulty receive as much attention as those of interpretation. At the end of the book is a full vocabulary list for all the words contained in the prescribed sections, with words in OCR's vocabulary list for AS Level Latin (www.ocr.org.uk/Images/72148-unit-f361-vocabulary-list-excel-version.xls) flagged by means of an asterisk.

In preparing this text I have been very much helped and supported by Alice Wright and her team at Bloomsbury. Christopher Tanfield, who is editing the A-Level Virgil text of *Aeneid* X, read all my notes with great care and improved them most substantially.

He and I worked together on the introduction to my great pleasure and benefit. James Morwood also read the notes and endeavoured to make sure that I kept the target readers in view. I must also say a warm thank you to the Fondation Hardt in Geneva for their hospitality over a period of the summer while I was working on *Aeneid* VIII.

Keith Maclennan

Introduction

The *Aeneid*

The *Aeneid* tells how Aeneas, of the royal house of Troy, escaped from the destruction of his city bearing his crippled father on his back and accompanied by his little son. He knew he was to seek a new home in the west. He did not know where this was to be. In the course of seven years travelling he followed many false trails, of which the most damaging was his stay in Carthage in North Africa. Driven there in a storm by the goddess Juno, he was sheltered by Carthage's queen, Dido, and allowed her to believe that he loved her and would stay there. She killed herself when he was obliged to leave. Before he reached his destination he was required to go to Hades to visit his now dead father, Anchises. There Anchises showed him a vision of glory: his descendants, the Romans, engaged in their mission of world conquest and pacification, which would reach its climax with the reign of Augustus. At last he reached the mouth of the river Tiber and understood that here was the place for the city he must found. He was also to unite his own people with the Latini, the existing occupants of the country, and marry the daughter of their king. But she was already committed to Turnus of the neighbouring Rutuli. Juno encouraged the development of a war between Aeneas' people and the Latini. There was great destruction and loss of life, including that of Pallas, the young son of a king who had become an ally of Aeneas. Aeneas' victory was not sealed until the last line of the poem, in which he refused Turnus mercy and killed him in revenge for Pallas.

The fourth-century commentator Servius stated confidently, 'This is Virgil's plan: to compose an imitation of Homer and to praise

Augustus through his ancestors.' There are many moments in the poem that represent Aeneas, and after him Rome and Augustus, in bright and encouraging colours. There are others in which Aeneas seems to be represented as a flawed hero. By his presentation of Aeneas struggling to fulfil his destiny, of the places he travels to, and of the gods and the people who confront or assist him on his way, Virgil created a world that fires the imagination and still provokes fierce controversy.

Rome before Augustus

The early 30s BCE, when Virgil was at the beginning of his career, were years of deep and justified pessimism for the Romans. Possessors of an enormous empire, rulers of almost every nation around the Mediterranean shores, and in some cases far beyond them, they were unable to provide peaceful and ordered government at home.

The problem stretched back for a century and more, and lay in the huge disruption caused by the change from city state to centre of empire. Between 202 and 133 BCE Greece, eastern Spain, southern France, Africa and territories in what is now Turkey fell under Roman control, largely by conquest. The profits of those conquests were very unevenly divided. This and other factors led to social and economic tension in Italy symbolised by the political murder of the reformer Tiberius Gracchus in 133. Later historians dated the civil wars from this point for a century until 31. In 106 a reform of the army turned it from an *ad hoc* muster of soldiers, expecting to serve for a campaign and then return home, to a professional force, dependent upon its commander for pay, booty and resettlement. From this point, it is not unreasonable to see Roman affairs as degenerating into a succession of competitions between warlords, each potential competitor striving to achieve the political authority that would allow him to command an army, using it for his own profit and to intimidate his opponents in Rome. In 50 BCE there were two such warlords, Julius Caesar and Pompeius Magnus. Caesar defeated Pompeius and his sons and supporters in a series of wars from 49 in Greece to 45 in Spain. Returning to Rome in early 44, Caesar had himself declared 'perpetual dictator', only to be murdered within a month in a conspiracy of political conservatives and supporters of Pompeius.

In the ensuing chaos, it was impossible to know where legitimate government lay. Power was contested between Caesar's leading follower, Mark Antony, the representatives of the old regime such as Brutus, Cassius and Cicero, and, suddenly appearing on the scene, Caesar's nineteen-year-old great nephew Octavian, adopted by Caesar in his will. A year of confusion, violence and bewildering changes of side (44–43) left Antony and Octavian combining to fight Brutus and Cassius. After their victory at Philippi in 42 the empire was divided up, falling ultimately into two halves, the West controlled by Octavian and the East controlled from Egypt by Antony. It was only a matter of time before Antony and Octavian were again in dispute, while from Spain, and then Sicily, a surviving son of Pompey still carried on his father's struggle until 36. Meanwhile Rome and Italy descended into chaos, banditry and frequent starvation. Finally in 31 Antony, with his supporter Cleopatra, Queen of Egypt, was defeated by Octavian at the naval battle of Actium. In 27 Octavian took the name 'Augustus'.

In the writings of this period there are several that lament the chaos and express the longing, sometimes in fantasy, for a saviour. In Virgil's 4th *Eclogue* (c. 41 BCE) the idea is expressed but the identity of the saviour is unclear. In the 1st *Eclogue* (c.38) there is a semi-divine young man who can hardly be anyone but Octavian. By the time of the *Georgics* (late 30s) it is 'Caesar' – i.e. Octavian – by name.

Virgil's life

Mantua me genuit, Calabri rapuere, tenet nunc
Parthenope; cecini pascua, rura, duces.

I was born in Mantua, died in Calabria, and lie buried in Naples. I was
a poet, and my poetry was pastoral, agricultural and epic.

The inscription on Virgil's tomb summarises his life and works. We
hear a little more than this, mostly thanks to a biography written
originally by the second-century writer Suetonius, though much of
the detail in this may be unreliable inference based on the assumption
that Virgil's poems contained autobiographical detail.

There is no reason to doubt the dates given for his birth – 15th
October 70 BCE – and his death – 21st September 19 BCE – or the
statement that he was born near Mantua in a part of modern Italy that
was at that date still administered as a province called Cisalpine Gaul
('Gaul this side of the Alps'). From his own poetry it is clear that he
had an education that included the whole range of writers, Greek and
Roman, available at the time.

The beginning of his poetic career has been dated to 'the age of 28',
i.e. 42–41 BCE, with the publication of pastoral poetry (commonly
known to us as *Eclogues*). This date is roughly confirmed by the fact
that the 4th *Eclogue* is dedicated to Asinius Pollio, military commander,
author of tragedies and founder of Rome's first public library. Virgil
speaks of his consulship as about to take place; it did so in 40. The
subject-matter of the *Eclogues* is centred round the activities of
shepherds in an idealised ('Arcadian') landscape, but the poems also
contain some remarkable references to the contemporary events:
Pollio's consulship, the brutal displacement of landowners for the
benefit of soldiers, the death of Julius Caesar.

The poems also show him as having patrons other than Pollio. By
the early 30s he had come to the attention of Maecenas, friend of

Octavian, the future Augustus. It was Maecenas for whom Virgil composed his next major work, the *Georgics*, ostensibly a handbook of farming in the ancient tradition of 'didactic' poetry, but containing, even more than the *Eclogues*, reference to his own times. Now in the late 30s Octavian was preparing for the contest that would bring him to absolute power, and in the *Georgics* are substantial passages praising Octavian and looking forward to his victory.

Some smaller poems, part of a collection known as the *Appendix Vergiliana*, which has been attributed to Virgil, suggest that at some time he retired from Rome in order to live as a member of a philosophical community in Naples. Among the papyrus fragments that have turned up in a splendid villa in Herculaneum, there is a reference to 'Varius and Vergilius and Quintilius'. Varius and Quintilius were well-known figures of literary life; they may well have been at the centre of intellectual life in Naples. But there is nothing to suggest 'retirement'.

According to the *Life*, Virgil had completed the *Georgics* by the time Octavian had defeated Antony and was on his way back to Rome in 29. Virgil is said to have read all four books to Octavian in his country home near Naples, with Maecenas taking over when Virgil became tired. He now embarked on the *Aeneid*, which was to occupy him for the rest of his life. He composed it, as the *Life* says, by making a twelve-book draft and then filling this in *particulatim*, 'bit by bit', i.e. as the fancy took him and not in order. Hence, no doubt, the presence of a good number of incomplete lines, where one completed bit comes up against another with the join not yet made. Octavian (who became 'Augustus' in January 27) is said to have become impatient with the slow progress of the work. Part of an apologetic but unrepentant letter from Virgil survives.

By 19 BCE the *Aeneid* was virtually complete. Virgil resolved to devote three years to its revision and travelled to Greece where he intended to carry this out. Augustus met him in Athens and persuaded him to return to Italy. He fell ill on the way and died at Brindisi on 21st September. He had said that he wished the uncompleted script to be burned, but Varius refused to carry out his wish and, with another friend Plotius Tucca, on Augustus' instructions, edited and published it.

Sources

Literary sources

In writing an epic Virgil was putting himself in a tradition that had started with Homer: the *Iliad*, about the decisive moments in the Trojan War, and the *Odyssey*, about the return from Troy of one of the Greek heroes to his home. Ancient scholars observed that the Aeneid could be divided into one half (I–VI) derived from Homer's *Odyssey* and one half (VII–XII) from his *Iliad*. Other divisions, not tied to Homer, have been suggested (e.g. I–IV, V–VIII, IX–XII), but the two-halves division is a useful one. At the beginning of Book VII Virgil describes the coming books as *maius opus* – 'a greater work' (VII.45). Many of the set pieces of these books are derived from the Iliad. Aspects of style are consistent with this, for example, the increased number of similes in VII–XII reflecting the much larger number of similes in the *Iliad* compared with the *Odyssey*.

Homer provides the basic structure and a huge amount of the detail, as any close reading will show. But everywhere in the *Aeneid* there is evidence of Virgil's wide use of other sources. Book II draws on epic poetry attributed to Homer but barely known to us (the 'epic cycle'): *Little Iliad*, *Iliu Persis* ('Sack of Troy'). The Dido episode is heavily influenced by the *Argonautica* by Apollonius Rhodius (third century BCE), and also by earlier Athenian tragedy (IV.469–73 the most obvious) and Catullus 64, a poem in which

Ariadne is deserted by Theseus. The Camilla episode in Book XI is inspired by the story of the Amazon Penthesilea recorded in the cyclic *Aethiopis*. Also in the background is Ennius, second-century BCE author of tragedies and an epic poem on Roman history (using the hexameter for the first time in Latin literature). With Lucretius' great philosophical poem *de Rerum Natura* Virgil was intimately familiar. Lucretius' poem justifies materialism and atheism. *Aen.* VI.724–751 is an astonishing passage where Virgil uses Lucretius' language to express the exact opposite.

It is a little intimidating to approach Virgil in the knowledge that there is this world of earlier literature behind him. It is important to understand that Virgil is not simply engaged in stealing his predecessors' good ideas: he pays us the compliment of inviting us to remember the passages to which he refers and to think of himself as having a discussion with them.

Aeneas as the forefather of Rome, and of Augustus

Aeneas appears in the *Iliad* as one of the leading Trojans. In *Il.* XX.273–308 he is in imminent danger of being killed by Achilles. The god Poseidon rescues him because of his piety and because it is fated that he should survive and originate a dynasty ruling over the Trojans. His story develops, and by the fifth century BCE it includes the idea that in escaping from Troy he rescued his little son and crippled father. His connection with Rome developed in the third century, in a period when contacts between Greece and Rome were growing. In an early version of the story Romulus was a son of Aeneas. Ennius' own version was not far from this: Ilia, the princess of Alba, mother of Romulus, was a daughter of Aeneas. This was (in mythical terms) a chronological impossibility: the traditional date for the fall of Troy was 1183 BCE, for the foundation of Rome, 753. To fill this gap Virgil makes use of two main traditions apparently then existing or developing:

i. Lavinium. The settlement was anciently the religious centre of the
Latin League, the confederation of which Rome was part, and
which was effectively absorbed into the Roman state after the war
that ended in 338 BCE. The religious symbols from the shrine of
Lavinium were named the *Penates populi Romani* ('household gods
of the Roman people') and identified with the *penates* brought from
Troy by Aeneas. Thus Aeneas can bring the *penates*, found
Lavinium and leave Romulus to found Rome itself much later.

ii. Alba Longa. Romulus was a member of the royal house of Alba.
Alba was founded from Lavinium by Aeneas' son Ascanius/Iulus.
Some of the most ancient families of Rome asserted a distant
origin in Troy and a more recent one in Alba; of these the most
conspicuous was that of Julius Caesar, claiming descent from Iulus.

Virgil's use of these traditions can be partly seen from the summary of
Books VII–XII (pp***). Aeneas is to marry Latinus' daughter Lavinia,
who will give her name to Lavinium. Iulus will found Alba Longa, of
whose royal house Romulus will be a member. But Iulus is the ancestor
of the Julii, not of the Alban kings, while the Alban kings are to be
descendants of Lavinia who has nothing to do with the foundation of
Alba. The solution to the problem lay in Silvius, a son of Aeneas and
Lavinia (*Aen.*VI.762). At some point (Virgil is vague; Livy skates
over the issue) Silvius takes over the kingship of Alba, thus creating
a separate Trojan ancestry for both Romulus and the Julii. This,
of course, lies in the future for Aeneas, so information given to him
(and us) comes in the veiled language of prophecy (*Aen.*I.267–77,
VI.760–6); it was evidently an unresolved issue in Augustan times.

Homer and *Aeneid* 8

In the *Odyssey* Books I–IV Odysseus' son Telemachus is prompted by
the goddess Athena to find news of his father. He travels by sea from his

home on the island of Ithaca to visit Odysseus' Trojan war colleagues, Nestor at Pylos and Menelaus at Sparta. In *Odyssey* XIII Odysseus himself lands at a remote spot in his home island of Ithaca. He is directed by his patron goddess Athena not to go straight home but to seek the help of his swineherd Eumaeus. Both these threads of narrative, as well as other events in the Homeric poems are woven by Virgil into his account of Aeneas' visit to Evander, and will be commented on at relevant points in the notes, as will some other Homeric references.

Virgil's style: a practical guide

A

What's the difference between prose and verse?

Lines 102–104:

> *Forte die sollemnem illo rex Arcas honorem*
> *Amphitryoniadae magno divisque ferebat*
> *ante urbem in luco.*

By chance that very day the Arcadian king was bringing a solemn offering to the great son of Amphitryon and the gods, outside the city in a grove.

Imagine this as a sentence presented in a standard prose style:

> *Illo die forte rex Arcas Herculi deisque ante urbem in luco sacrificabat.*

By chance the Arcadian king was sacrificing to Hercules that day in a grove outside the city.

For *sacrificabat* Virgil has used a relatively elaborate phrase *sollemnem honorem ferebat*, making use of the abstract noun *honorem*, establishing the importance of the ceremony.

Illo follows *die* with which it agrees; *sollemnem* comes before *honorem* with which it agrees, and the two phrases interlock so as to create a single phrase. *Arcas* is the third adjectival word here; it is the only one to go immediately next to its noun, sandwiched inside the complex formed by the other two phrases. The line is thus tightly held together. *Illo*, delayed until after its noun, carries the stress: 'on that very day'.

For *Herculi* Virgil has given us a grand epic-style patronymic. For *deis* he gives us the archaic *divis*. The result is a four-word line, rare and imposing (there are only three such in our passage of Book VIII).

Lines 102 and 103 are metrically similar, but not identical. We notice that both lines are divided at a fourth-foot caesura and that the first parts rhyme with each other.

The place phrase *ante urbem in luco*, a heavy, spondaic phrase with two elisions, is put conspicuously at the end of the sentence, outside the tightly knitted unit preceding them, after the verb and at the beginning of a line, breaking off half-way through the line – and once again, rhyming. This is deliberate; the exact location of the ceremony is important: the Ara Maxima.

The rhymes, the epic words, the spondaic conclusion combine to make the effect of these lines solemn and ponderous – deliberately so.

Note that **adjectives** create patterns as above and in such self-contained lines as:

197 *(A) ora virum (b) tristi pendebant (a) pallida (B) tabo*
     men's faces were hanging, blanched with horrid decay

(upper case representing a noun and lower case an adjective), or:

235 *(a) dirarum nidis (B) domus (b) opportuna (A) volucrum*
     a suitable home for the nests of ill-omened birds

though neither of these is an instance of the 'Golden Line' (a name given currency by the poet Dryden), *abAB*. For example:

43 *(a) litoreis (b) ingens inventa sub (A) ilicibus (B) sus*
a huge sow, discovered beneath the coastal holm-oaks.

Style tells a story

Lines 228–232:

*Ecce / fúrens ánimis / áderat Tirynthius / omnémque
accéssum lústrans / huc ora ferebat et illuc, /
dentibus infréndens. / tér tótum fervidus ira
lustrat Aventini montem, / ter saxea temptat
limina / nequiquam, / ter fessus valle resedit.*

See, raging in fury the Tirynthian was there, and viewing every approach he kept turning his face this way and that, grinding his teeth. Thrice, boiling with anger, he views the whole of the Aventine hill; thrice he attempts the rock-built gateway, in vain; thrice he sank back wearily in the valley.

The obliques indicate suggested pauses in a reading (not all of equal length). Accents are placed on syllables that seem to require particular stress.

i.   *Ecce*: with this word the narrator (Virgil/Evander) invites us/ Aeneas not just to listen to him, but to be present in the scene.
ii. *animi*: pl. means 'anger' (OLD 11), so in the abl.: 'in anger', thus duplicating the idea in *furens*.
iii. The first three feet in line 228 are all dactyls, and the word stresses, as indicated, clash violently with the verse-stress; the point made more evident by having the third and fourth words begin with the same letter. Hercules races up the hill.
iv. *Tirynthius*: another grand word for Hercules; it suddenly slows the line down with its long syllables.
v.   The next phrase is even slower, ignoring the line end and, very unusually, containing a superfluous syllable. Although this syllable virtually disappears by elision in the reading, it

probably has the effect of casting the word-accent onto the *e* of *omnem*, thereby disrupting the normal pattern, and in this spondaic passage putting a stress (verse- or word-) on every syllable from *omn-* to *-ans*, thereby slowing up the words and illustrating Hercules' frustrated search at the top of the hill.

vi. *lustrans*: the verb is originally a ritual term, 'pass over' for the purpose of purifying. In its non-ritual sense it is largely poetic; it carries the idea of 'viewing thoroughly'. The repetition of the word in line 231 is striking: it perhaps conveys something of the impatience and anger with which one looks for missing objects two and three times in the same place.

vii. *ora ferebat*: for this *circumspiciebat* would be the routine prose term. The word *ora* has just a hint of artificiality: it is pl. for sing. The plural creates a short syllable; Latin hexameter poets needed all of these they could get. But the phrase *ora ferebat* gives a vivid sense of Hercules' head and eyes turning.

viii. *huc* and *illuc*: these words are stressed by being placed at the beginning and end of the phrase.

ix. *dentibus infrendens*: Hercules' open lips and grinding teeth are illustrated by the repeated *e*-sounds, *d*, *t*, and double consonants introduced by *n*. (Note also the rolled *r*; the letter was described by the satirist Persius as *canina* 'doggy'; whatever exactly he meant, there was surely an element of growling ferocity.)

x. *ter ... ter ... ter*: the phrases are connected by the repeated word which also hammers home Hercules' repeated efforts.

xi. *totum* with *montem*: there is nowhere to pause between these words; the phrase disrupts the sequence of lines, as with *omnem ... lustrans*.

xii. *nequiquam*: adverbs usually come *before* their verbs. This one is a big word, coming well *after* its verb *temptat*. It puts a strong emphasis on Hercules' frustration.

xiii. *lustrat . . . temptat . . . resedit*: The first two of these verbs are (historic) present; the last is perfect. Virgil could have continued the sequence of present tenses with *residit*. Why didn't he? Is the transition from vivid present to narrative perfect deflating?

B

Not all discussions of 'style' should be concerned with such minutiae. Fine details are important, but so are, among others, the following issues. For any passage, it is worth asking the following (overlapping) questions.

i. **Pace.** Is the narrative moving quickly (so that you find yourself having to supply details from your imagination), or slowly (there are more details than seem strictly necessary). Why has Virgil chosen to leave out or include details?

ii. **Tone.** What is the tone of the passage? Is it detached? Relaxed? Intense? Concentrated? Discursive? Ironic? Literal? Didactic? Serious? Humorous?

iii. **Focalisation.** From whose (if anyone's) point of view is the story being told? Especially, where a character is speaking, is there reason to think that this represents a private point of view or one that others (including the reader) might not share?

iv. **Structure.** How does this passage relate (a) to the section of the narrative of which it is part, (b) to the story as a whole?

v. **Intertextuality.** Is there anything to suggest that Virgil is making a conscious – or unconscious – reference to another work? If so, what does it add to our understanding of this text?

Using the questions listed above, let us consider lines 86–96:

> *Thybris ea fluvium, quam longa est, nocte tumentem*
> *leniit, et tacita refluens ita substitit unda*
> *mitis ut in morem stagni placidaeque paludis*

sterneret aequor aquis, remo ut luctamen abesset.
ergo iter inceptum celerant rumore secundo: 90
labitur uncta vadis abies; mirantur et undae,
miratur nemus insuetum fulgentia longe
scuta virum fluvio pictasque innare carinas.
olli remigio noctemque diemque fatigant,
et longos superant flexus, variisque teguntur   95
arboribus, viridesque secant placido aequore silvas.

That night, for its whole length, Tiber calmed his flood and, as he retreated, came to so complete a stop, with his stream now quiet, that he laid a flat surface on his waters, like a calm lake and a placid pool, so that there should be no effort for the oar. So they speed their passage once started to cries of encouragement. The waxed fir glides through the water; even the waves are amazed, and the woods too, unfamiliar (with the sight) are amazed at the warriors' shields gleaming afar and (amazed) that painted ships are afloat on the river. Those (warriors) tire the night and the day with rowing and pass long reaches and are sheltered under all kinds of trees and on the placid water they cut (their way through) the green woods.

i.   **Pace.** Virgil devotes three lines to the river being 'calm', then six lines to the idea of 'easily and pleasantly'. The Tiber plays a big part in Aeneas' eventual arrival in Italy, with a delightful scene at its estuary (VII.29–34), a careful description of the god himself (VIII.31–4) and a substantial and instructive speech (VIII.36–65). The beauty of the scene (as seen through Aeneas' eyes) seems designed to make him feel 'at home' and in the care of the gods.

ii. **Tone.** The tone is relaxed, as the narrator encourages his audience to enjoy a scene as he and his characters enjoy it. The relaxed spirit is evident in the syntax of the last sentence: no climax, just four separate sentences one after the other joined by *et* and *-que*.

iii. **Focus.** The passage also includes a charming change of focus: in 91–3 it is the woods and river that enjoy the presence of the ships; in 94–6 it is the sailors who enjoy the woods and the river.

iv. **Structure.** Much more than in Homer, each book of the *Aeneid* is a self-contained unit. Within those units, divisions are less hard and fast. The whole passage 81–305 can be seen as 'The Hercules Story', though within it lines 169–171 point ominously towards the next stage. To that story these lines (up to 101) form an introduction.

v. **Intertextuality.** Virgil's readers are also invited to feel at home, by the hints of traditional epic, i.e. Ennius, in *labitur uncta* (91), and the old-fashioned *olli* (94).

C

Finally the simile, that element of style crucial to Virgil, one of the essential elements of epic poetry, inherited from Homer along with the hexameter verse and the concern with gods and heroes.

A very few similes in Virgil are brief suggestions: in *Aen*.I.82 the winds rush out *velut agmine facto* like an advancing army. Almost all are lengthier ('extended similes'), creating a picture independent of their surroundings. Here again is a suggested approach to consideration of these.

i. Exactly what in the narrative does the simile seem to illustrate? There may well be more than one answer to this.

ii. When you have taken from the text of the simile all the points which come under (i), what is left? Consider whether this has any more general bearing on the development of the epic. (It is one of the arguments advanced by Oliver Lyne (*Words and the Poet*, p.72) that some similes effectively continue the narrative, or fill in gaps in it.)

iii. Is there any 'cross-fertilisation'? Has any language appropriate to the story, but not the simile, crept into the simile or vice versa? If so, is it important for the narrative as a whole?

A brief example from Book II is given below. For an example in Book VIII, see lines 243-6 and pp. 70-1 in the Commentary.

In Book II lines 354-60 Aeneas is encouraging a group of young men to storm through Troy, killing as many Greeks as they can in a desperate act of revenge:

> *una salus victis nullam sperare salutem.*
> *sic animis iuvenum furor additus.* inde, lupi ceu   355
> raptores atra in nebula, quos improba ventris
> exegit caecos rabies, catulique relicti
> faucibus exspectant siccis, *per tela, per hostes*
> *vadimus haud dubiam in mortem, mediaeque tenemus*
> *urbis iter. nox atra cava circumvolat umbra.*   360

Do not hope to survive! It is your only hope of survival. This added fury to their youthful courage. Then, like ravening wolves, under a black cover of mist, driven blind by the insistent madness of the belly, whose abandoned cubs are waiting with parched jaws, we stride through missiles and through enemies to certain death, and we take the road for the middle of the city. Black night covers us round with its wings of hollow darkness.

i.   The main point of contact is *furor*, which is picked up by the *rabies* of the wolves.

ii. *Atra in nebula* looks at first sight like a rhetorical touch of colour, until we see that it has crept in from outside the simile (360). Nevertheless it contributes to the blindness (357) of the wolves, and points to the blindness of Aeneas and his gang. *Ventris rabies* (356-7) is the irresistible force for the wolves; for the men it is the *furor* of 355.

iii. What of the *catuli*? To begin with they seem a very colourful, but optional, extra. But for the wolves they are part of the force that makes them hunt. Are the men under any such pressure? It will not be long before Aeneas is reminded by Venus that his first duty is to care for his family at home. Very neatly, this idea has been stealthily inserted in what seems a passage of black and relentless fury.

D

The above discussion has avoided technical terms except for those of metre, on the grounds that it is much more important to read Virgil than to label him. But labels serve a purpose, and here is a list of generally useful ones. It could be a good exercise to see which, if any, of these labels is appropriate to each of the points above.

alliteration, assonance Use of these terms is not fixed hard and fast. It is suggested that 'alliteration' is used for an effect created by initial repeated sounds (e.g. 88: *mitis ut in morem stagni placidaeque paludis*) and 'assonance' for an effect created by repeated sounds in other contexts (i.e. 230 *dentibus infrendens* (see above)).

anacoluthon When the syntax of a sentence is interrupted, e.g. 'If you cross the road now – but the lights have changed.' (565–6n.)

anaphora Connection of sentences/phrases not by a conjunction or particle but by repetition of a word at the beginning, e.g. *ter* in 230–2.

apostrophe When the author addresses one of his own characters, e.g. VIII.643: *at tu dictis, Albane, maneres* ('But you should have stood by your word, man of Alba.').

apposition A grammatical construction in which two elements, normally nouns or noun phrases, are understood together, with one element serving to identify the other in a different way: 134 *Dardanus, Iliacae pater urbis:* 'Dardanus, father of the Trojan city'.

archaic, archaism Use of a word or phrase outdated by the time a piece is written, e.g. 127: *Graiugenum* for standard *Graiugenarum*.

assonance See 'alliteration'.

asyndeton When parallel expressions have no connecting word, e.g. 'She starts, she moves, she seems to feel / The thrill of life along her keel'; 246: *cernatur, trepident.* Cf. **polysyndeton**.

chiasmus Where a second phrase repeats the first in its overall structure, but reverses the component parts (AB,BA), e.g. 'The oranges are for you;

for me the apples.' See 271–2: (A) *quae maxima semper* (B) *dicetur . . . et*
(B) *erit* (A) *quae maxima semper* ('which will always be *called* 'greatest'
and which will *be* greatest').

ecphrasis (a) A description of a work of art, such as the shield at the end of
Book VIII, or (b) more generally, a self-contained descriptive passage
often creating a pause in the action.

enjambment When the sense continues over the line-end. This may have a
relatively weak effect, as in 119–20 *lectos / Dardaniae venisse duces* ('[tell
him that] chosen leaders of Troy have come'), or a strong one, as in
238–9 *inde repente / impulit* ('Then suddenly he struck it').

epiphonema A brief sentence (often a single line) to wind up a passage, e.g.
101: *ocius advertunt proras urbique propinquant.* 'Promptly they turn
their bows and come near to the city'.

hendiadys When a single idea is presented as if it were two separate ones,
e.g. 225: *ferro et arte paterna* ('by iron and his father's skill' = by his
father's skill in ironworking).

hypallage or **transferred epithet** In 525 *Tyrrhenusque tubae clangor,* ('the
Etruscan bray of the trumpet') the adjective Etruscan is 'transferred' from
'trumpet' to 'bray'; the phrase means 'the bray of the Etruscan trumpet'.

hyperbaton From a Greek word meaning 'transgression'. (a) When a word is
displaced into a phrase that is not its own, e.g. 168: *frenaque bina meus quae
nunc habet aurea Pallas* ('two golden bits which my Pallas now possesses').
Aurea agrees with *frena*, so comes unexpectedly inside the *quae* clause;
meus with Pallas, so unexpectedly outside it. (b) When an epithet agrees
with its noun across intervening words, e.g. 230 *totum* agrees with 231
montem. (Of course 168 *meus* and *aurea* are covered by this definition too.)

hyperbole Exaggeration, e.g. 99–100: *caelo aequavit* ('. . . has put on a level
with heaven') of the Palatine hill.

hysteron proteron A Greek term meaning 'the later earlier.' When two
events are referred to in reverse order, e.g. 201: *auxilium adventumque
dei* ('. . . the help and arrival of a god'); the god must arrive before he
helps. (But see note on line 201, p. 64.)

litotes When less is said than is meant, e.g. X.494: *haud illi stabunt Aeneia parvo
hospitia:* (Evander) 'will not find himself paying a small price for having
entertained Aeneas. . . .' (No: the price will be huge: the death of his son.)

metaphor Use of a term appropriate for one context in another, e.g. 93: of ships *innare* 'to swim' (involving personification of the ships).

metonymy When something is referred to not as itself but as something recognisably associated with it, e.g. 181: *Bacchumque ministrant* (They serve the wine). 'Wine' is given the name of its patron god.

onomatopoeia The use of words that seem to imitate the sounds they refer to, e.g. 230: *dentibus infrendens* (as above, p.12).

parataxis When ideas are expressed as independent of one another and the connexion is made by the reader/listener, e.g. 'She saw the fire. She ran into the house. She rescued the child.' When the connexion is made by the words themselves we have '**hypotaxis**', i.e. 'Seeing the fire, she ran into the house to rescue the child.' (Compare the hypotactic style of 225–30 with the paratactic style of 175–8.)

periphrasis When more words are used than are strictly necessary for communication, e.g. VIII.68–9: *aetherii spectans orientia solis lumina:* 'gazing at *the rising light of the heavenly sun*' for 'gazing at *the sunrise*'.

personification When inanimate objects are treated as animate, e.g. 240: *refluitque exterritus amnis* (the river flowed backwards in terror).

polyptoton When different parts (cases, tenses etc.) of the same word are used in a deliberate sequence, e.g. 185: *haec sollemnia . . ., has . . . dapes, hanc . . . aram* ('these rites, this festivity, this altar'). Here used as a connection, very like anaphora.

polysyndeton When every component of a list is joined by a conjunction, e.g. 94–6 *-que, -que, et, -que, -que*.

prolepsis, adj. **proleptic** A Greek term meaning 'anticipation'. When an idea is presented in narrative before it becomes true, e.g. 260–1: *angit . . . siccum sanguine guttur.* ('He squeezed his dry-of-blood throat' = 'he squeezed his throat till it was dry . . .')

simile An (often extensive) comparison, e.g. 243–6: Cacus' dwelling with the world of the dead.

synchysis From Greek meaning 'confusion', 'muddle'. When natural word-order is altered for effect. Both types of hyperbaton are instances of synchysis, and cf. 272 *erit quae maxima semper* for *quae maxima semper erit* ('. . . which will always be the greatest').

synecdoche When the term for a part of something is used for the whole. In 44 *capita* (heads) is used to refer to individual young pigs.

theme and variation When an idea is repeated in different words, e.g. 171: *auxilio laetos dimittam opibusque iuvabo*: 'I shall send (them) away contented with my help and support (them) with my resources'.

transferred epithet See **hypallage**.

tricolon A group of three parallel expressions, often growing towards the last ('tricolon crescens'), e.g. 'I came, I saw, I conquered.' See 201–3, note. And for a tricolon 'diminuens', see 230–2.

Rhythm and Metre

Metrical pattern

Traditionally, lines of verse have a predictable rhythm created by the pattern of stressed and unstressed syllables:

> The King sits in Dunfermline town
>> Drinking the blood-red wine.
> 'Oh where will I find a skeely skipper
>> To sail this new ship o' mine?'

> Half hour, half hour from Aberdour
>> 'Tis forty fathoms deep,
> And there lies good Sir Patrick Spens
>> Wi' the Scots lords at his feet.

There is a strong rhythm about these lines: stressed syllables alternate with unstressed syllables; each line begins with an unstressed syllable; four-stress lines alternate with three-stress lines.

Words and metre

Yet the above is an over-simplification. Although the rhythm is there, it would be silly to say line 1 stressing 'in' or line 2 stressing '-ing', and, once this is accepted, it becomes clear that there is great flexibility in the way the words can be said. Two syllables take the place of one ('skipper', 'wi' the'); rhythmically unstressed syllables must be given as much weight as stressed syllables ('blood-red', 'half-hour', 'Scots lords') and so on. So that, although *the rhythm is created by the natural accent of the words*, it has its own independent existence, and there are two principles, 'meaning' and 'rhythm', in an interesting competition with each other.

Latin metre

Long and short syllables

The same 'competition' exists in Latin verse as in English. The difference is that in Latin *the rhythm is created by the pattern of long and short syllables*.

It seems that in Latin long and short syllables were more sharply and systematically differentiated than they are in English. To understand Latin metre it is necessary to recognise 'quantity' (i.e. whether a syllable is long or short). A 'short' syllable is equal to half the length of a 'long' syllable. Here are the basic guidelines. (For a fuller exploration, see NLG 5, 362–4.)

- A syllable is long if:

  - it contains a diphthong (i.e. two vowels pronounced together as one syllable, e.g. 'æger').
  - it contains a naturally long vowel. *Māter* has a long 'a', *păter* a short; *rēges* 'kings' a long first *e*; *rĕges* 'you will rule' a short. Sometimes the length of a vowel is a clue to the inflection of the word: thus 'puellă' is nominative or vocative, 'puellā' ablative. Many Latin dictionaries mark naturally long vowels.
  - it contains a naturally short vowel followed by two consonants, whether in the same word or split between words. Thus, in 'ĕt

clĭpĕūm' (line 242), the 'e' of 'et' is naturally short but is
lengthened by position. 'x' or 'z' are in themselves double-
consonants. A consonant followed in the same word by 'l' or 'r'
gives the poet the option to treat a previous short vowel as long
– thus 'ăgrōs' or 'āgrōs'. 'h' is ignored. An 'i' can be a consonant
or a vowel. In *iacit* 'he throws', a two-syllable word, the first *i*
is a consonant sounding 'y', the second a vowel. 'qu' counts as
a single consonant; so does 'su' in a very few contexts: *suavis,
suesco.*

- A syllable is short if it contains a naturally short vowel followed
  by a single consonant or another vowel pronounced separately
  (e.g. 'pŭella').

Metre based on quantity: the hexameter

Complicated as they sound, the rules quickly become second nature.
From them metrical schemes were developed. For epic poetry, both
Greek and Roman, the standard was the **dactylic hexameter**: 'dactylic'
because based around the 'dactyl' pattern of $-\cup\cup$ ('daktylos' in Greek
means 'finger' – look at the joints on the index finger of your left hand,
palm towards you); and 'hexameter' because there are six dactylic
'feet'. For the first four of these feet, a 'spondee' ($- -$) could replace
the dactyl, while the last foot is either a 'trochee' ($-\cup$) or a spondee,
since the last syllable can be of indeterminate length (*syllaba anceps*).
The fifth is almost always a dactyl:

1	2	3	4	5	6
$-\ \cup\cup$	$-\ \cup\cup$	$-\ \cup\cup$	$-\ \cup\cup$	$-$	$-\ \cup$
$-$	$-$	$-$	$-$	$\cup\cup$	$-$

We 'scan' line 91 thus:

lābĭtŭr | ūnctă vă | dīs ăbĭ | ēs; mī | rāntŭr ĕt | ūndǣ

When a vowel/diphthong, or a vowel followed by an '-m', at the end of a word encounters a vowel or 'h-' at the start of the next word, that final syllable is **elided**, i.e. ignored from the point of view of scansion. It would probably have been pronounced, but in an understated way that allowed the metre to rumble on. It does not happen across line endings. Here are lines 163–4 with the elided syllables bracketed.

> ... *Anchis | es. mihi | mens iuve | nal(i) ard | ebat amore*
> *compel | lare vir(um) | et dex | trae con | iungere | dextram.*

Some elisions are more intrusive than others. Virgil exploits this in the example above, where the last syllable of a phrase (*-um*) is elided against the first syllable of the following phrase, thereby hurrying the words along and creating a sense of urgency. Sometimes, again for effect, the poet may choose not to elide (the scansion tells you this); so-called **hiatus** can be expressive or just mark a pause between clauses (none in our section of VIII, but e.g. in I.617 there is a very unusual line-ending *Dārdănĭ | ō Ănch | īsaē*).

Words and metre: competition (see (b) in Latin)

Even before you consider the words and what they mean, the metre allows for great variety in the sound of each line. Think of the words as well, and the variety is immensely increased. The metre suggests six stresses (the **ictus**), one on the first syllable of each foot. But each word has its own natural stress (the **accent**), which depends on the quantity of the *second-last syllable*. If this is short, the accent falls on the third-last syllable (*régimus*); if long, or if there are only two syllables, on the second-last (*régit, regēbat*). In the presence of both ictus and accent (see further below) lies much of the 'competition'.

'Caesura' and 'diaeresis'

In this competition it matters where word-divisions come. A word-break coinciding with the end of a foot is called **diaeresis**. A word break inside a foot is called **caesura**, 'strong' if after the first syllable, 'weak' if between the two shorts of a dactyl. There is a marked tendency for there to be a strong caesura in the third foot; if not there, in the second and fourth foot (or at least one of them). Caesura and diaeresis sometimes mark a break in the meaning as well as the rhythm (after *Graiugenum* 127, *impulit* 239), often not (after *Iliacae* 134, where the sense carries on to *urbis*, after *viscera* 180 below).

Ictus and Accent

Friénds, Rómans, coúntrymen, lénd me your eárs.

Above is an example of ictus (marked with underlining) in marked clash with accent (marked with acute).

I cóme to búry Caésar, nót to praíse him.

Here, however, ictus coincides with accent throughout.

In Virgil:

víscera tósta férunt taurór(um), onerántque canístris (180)

Here ictus (marked with underlining) coincides with accent (marked with acute) in five places, which is rather rare. The effect is perhaps an imitation of Homer.

In contrast:

quin ómn(em) Hespériam pénitus súa sub iúga míttant (148)

There is only one place in the whole line above where they coincide (sixth foot). This is very rare: it is almost invariable for ictus and accent to coincide in both fifth and sixth feet. It seems to be used here to express indignation.

Other effects such as the following exploit the fixedness of the line ending.

(i) **End-stopping/enjambment.** If sense and lines end together (end-stopping, e.g 131–5), the verse sounds more ordered; if the sense ends at different points from one line to another and not at the end (enjambment, e.g. 135–6), the effect is often one of effort.

(ii) **Spondaic fifth foot.** This is usually an allusion to another poet's work, e.g. 167 with on line note.

(iii) **Hypermetric line.** An extra syllable in the sixth foot elides against the first syllable of the following line. It can be used, like enjambment, to create a feeling of overflow and to change the stress-pattern at the end of the line, e.g. 228.

(iv) **Bucolic diaeresis.** This break in the sense at the end of the fourth foot, is so called because ancient grammarians associated it with Greek bucolic, i.e. pastoral poetry. See, e.g. 198.

(v) **Monosyllabic line ending.** This disrupts the coincidence of ictus and word accent in the fifth and sixth feet, e.g. just before our passage in line 83:

procubuit viridique in litore conspicitur sus.

The effect is archaic: here the reference seems to be to Lucretius.

There are additional details of metre discussed in individual style notes. There are some other terms (see also NLG 366–7) that you will meet in this edition:

(vi) **Brevis in longo.** A short syllable appearing in a place that would normally be occupied by a long syllable, e.g. 98 *procŭl* (see note).

(vii) **Syncope.** This is not strictly a metrical term, but a phenomenon caused by the exigencies of metre; a form of the verb that would be cumbersome is abbreviated, e.g. line 279, *optastis* for *optavistis.*

(viii) **Synizesis.** Where two successive vowels in the interior of a
word are scanned together as one, e.g. 194: *sēmihŏmĭnis.*

It cannot be emphasised too much that you must read out loud. Virgil's
verse is immensely expressive but that does not come across if it is
imprisoned on the page.

Book VIII

The Aeneid so far (figures in brackets refer to individual books):
(I) Aeneas has nearly reached Italy but is blown off course to Carthage
by a storm raised by Juno. He is welcomed by Queen Dido and entertained
at a feast during which he tells the stories of (II) the fall of Troy and (III)
his travels. (IV) Dido, partly at Venus' instigation, falls in love with him,
expecting him to stay with her in Carthage. Aeneas welcomes this state
of affairs until he is ordered by Jupiter through Mercury to leave. Dido
regards this as desertion, curses Aeneas and kills herself. (V) Aeneas'
voyage takes him to Sicily, where he holds funeral games for his father
Anchises who died there the year before. (VI) He lands in Italy at Cumae
from where the prophet-priestess of Apollo escorts him down to the
underworld. There he meets Anchises, who shows him a host of great
Romans who will be born in the future, culminating in Augustus. (VII)
His journey ends at the mouth of the Tiber with the fulfilment of a
prophecy about his destination. He has friendly discussions with the
local king Latinus, who decides to marry his daughter to Aeneas and not
to her Italian suitor Turnus. Juno refuses to allow matters to be so settled
and through the Fury Allecto stirs up war.

Aeneas has not been mentioned since early in Book VII. Developments
since then have been beyond his control. Late at night he falls asleep
on the river bank where he has been wrestling with the problems

facing him. The river-god of the Tiber comes to him in a dream with encouragement in two forms. In the morning he will experience the fulfilment of a prophecy made to him by his cousin Helenus (III.389–393): when he finds beside the river a white sow with her young to the number of thirty, this will mark the end of his wanderings and the place where he is to found his city. Further, he is to travel upriver to Pallanteum, a city founded by the Greek Evander and constantly at war with the Latins. Through Evander Aeneas is to gain the support he so much needs.

(66) Morning comes. It is as Tiber has said. Aeneas sacrifices the sow and her young to Juno, as instructed, and sails with his men to Pallanteum. Their voyage is made easy and delightful by the river-god. As they near the little city, they see its scattered roofs and its fortified strongpoint. This is the settlement that will become the city of Rome, and, with a brief comment from Virgil on the contrast between the place 'then' and 'now', it enters his story. Aeneas remains unaware of its significance.

(102) At Pallanteum the arrival of the Trojans in two warships causes alarm to begin with, but Aeneas convinces Evander of his peaceful intentions. He knows of Evander's ancestry and is able to show that he and Evander are related through their common descent from the giant Atlas. He hopes that this common descent, along with their shared interest in defeating the Latins, will be a satisfactory basis for alliance.

(152) Evander's response is warm and encouraging. From when he was a very young man he remembers meeting Aeneas' father Anchises and forming a close attachment to him. At that time he received from Anchises gifts that created a still-surviving bond of hospitality. He will do all he can to help. Meanwhile, the Trojans are to join him in his city's celebration of the annual festival in honour of Hercules.

(184) This festival commemorates the occasion when Hercules passed through Pallanteum on his way back from the lands of the

west. He had carried out there one of the Labours imposed upon him by Eurystheus king of Tiryns, killing the three-bodied giant Geryon and acquiring his cattle. Some of these cattle were stolen at Pallanteum by Cacus, a monstrous fire-breathing creature that lived on the Aventine Hill. Hercules tracked his cattle down to Cacus' cave, broke it open from above and killed the monster. There is an altar dedicated to Hercules round which the festival takes place. Only now are we told something of which Virgil's audience will already have been well aware, that this is the great altar – the *Ara Maxima* – which in Virgil's day was a feature of the Forum Boarium, the 'Cattle Market', situated at just the point where Aeneas would come ashore.

(280) Evening is now coming on, and the feasting is resumed. A hymn in praise of Hercules is sung: how he strangled Juno's snakes in his cradle; how he sacked the cities of Troy and Oechalia; how he performed his Labours – killing the Centaurs, the Cretan bull, the Nemean lion – kidnapping Cerberus from the Underworld; fighting for the gods against the giants; outwitting the Lernaean Hydra; above all, defeating Cacus. When the feast is over, Evander takes Aeneas into his city. As they walk towards his home on the Palatine Hill, Evander tells Aeneas of the past history of Pallanteum: originally woodlands, the home of Fauns and Nymphs, the country was settled and organised by Jupiter's father Saturn, who came to Italy when driven out of Olympus by his son. Saturn's rule was a golden age, succeeded by invasions, wars and many changes of name, until Evander came at the direction of Apollo and Evander's prophetess-mother Carmentis. They walk past the Porta Carmentalis, named after her. They are now in the Velabrum, the space between the Capitol and the Palatine. From here Evander points leftward to the woods on the Capitol, which becomes Romulus' *Asylum,* and rightward to the Lupercal, the sacred cave at the foot of the Palatine, the place where Romulus and Remus will in time be suckled by the she-wolf. Walking between the two hills

into what will be the Forum, Aeneas sees the Argiletum, the street leading out of it on the far side, and hears the mythical story of its name: *letum Argi* – 'the death of Argus'. He is then shown the Tarpeian Rock, the Capitol itself, and two ruined hill-top settlements, Janiculum and Saturnia. Passing through the Forum and the Carinae with their grazing cattle, they go up the Palatine by the side opposite to the Ara Maxima and reach Evander's house, which is evidently in the same place as Augustus', on the Cermalus, the north-west corner of the Palatine. This house is a humble affair, but Hercules once stayed there, and Aeneas, says Evander, should not despise it.

(370) The scene shifts to heaven. Venus persuades her husband Vulcan to make Aeneas armour for the forthcoming battle against the Rutuli and the Latins. Vulcan cannot resist her allurements, as he shows by extravagant comments such as 'For you I would have made sure Troy survived for another ten years'. After a night with Venus he gets up early and goes to his forge under Mount Etna in Sicily, where he instructs his three smiths, giant Cyclopes, to abandon all their other work (even thunderbolts for Jupiter) and make Aeneas his armour. There is a vivid description of a forge in full noisy action.

(454) Aeneas and Evander themselves now get up, accompanied by a very different sound: birdsong. There follows a four-man conference: Aeneas, Achates, Evander and Pallas. Evander explains that his own resources are inadequate to help Aeneas, but that that there is hope from the Etruscans. The citizens of Caere were for many years ruled by Mezentius, a brutal tyrant. When they managed to expel him, he took refuge with the Rutuli. Other Etruscans have sided with the Caeretans in wishing to make war on the Rutuli, but are prevented by oracles that say they will only succeed if they make a foreigner their leader. Aeneas can be the one. Evander will provide his own small contingent of 200 cavalry and send Pallas with them. As Aeneas and Achates hesitate over their response to this, Venus sends an omen: thunder and a vision of armour in a clear sky. Aeneas, with a confidence

that he has never shown before, acknowledges the omen and accepts Evander's offer. After sacrifice Aeneas divides his forces, some to return downriver, some to accompany him to Caere.

(554) The news that a cavalry detachment is on its way with all speed to the Etruscan king's palace gets out very shortly and flies around the little town. Anxious mothers redouble their prayers; fear grows with the danger, and larger now looms the spectre of war.

(558) Evander is in great distress, wishing that he still had the strength, as once he did, to go into battle, if only to keep his son safe. He bids Pallas farewell. In high confidence, Pallas now leaves with Aeneas on the way to Caere in Etruria. There, in a secluded valley, Aeneas receives his armour from Venus. The most conspicuous item is a huge shield, on which are pictured many of the great events of Roman history, whose climax, illustrated in gold and silver, is the Battle of Actium with Augustus at its centre. Also pictured is the triple triumph celebrated by Augustus in 29 BCE. Aeneas puts on this armour with pride, though he is unaware of what it foretells.

Hercules, Cacus and the Ara Maxima

Two terms may come in useful in discussing this passage.

Aition

Greek for 'cause', with the related English adjective 'aetiological'. Aetiological stories are those told in the form of mythological tales explaining why something in the present day is as it is. The *Aeneid* as a whole is an *aition* on a grand scale, explaining why Rome has the history it has had. Individual parts of the *Aeneid* are *aitia*: how Cape Misenum got its name (VI.212–235); why Carthage and Rome were enemies (IV.612–629). Here the story is partly an *aition*: why is the Ara Maxima important?

Epyllion

This term is used to refer to a short narrative in epic style either as a self-standing poem or as a part of a longer (epic) poem. A conspicuous example of the former is Catullus 64, 'The Marriage of Peleus and Thetis', of the latter Virgil *Georgic* IV.453–566, 'Orpheus and Eurydice'. Here 'Hercules and Cacus'.

Book VIII is arranged around three set pieces: the story of Hercules and Cacus, Aeneas' visit to the site of Rome, and the illustrations on the great shield. Each of them in their different ways establishes a connection between Virgil's day and the remote (or, in the case of some elements of the shield, not so remote) past. The story of Hercules and Cacus is focused on the Ara Maxima, a location very familiar to any inhabitant of Rome.

The Ara Maxima lay in the Forum Boarium, the Cattle Market, between the foot of the Palatine Hill and the Aventine, 'just behind the gateways of the Circus Maximus' according to Servius. There were several temples to Hercules in the area of the Forum Boarium, but the Ara Maxima seems always to have been a self-standing altar, and perhaps not a very conspicuous one in itself, given that archaeology has not identified any remains that can be confidently attributed to it. There was all the same something very special about it. It was ancient, dating back, according to tradition, long before the foundation of the city. Ceremonies there were conducted according to a Greek ritual, and it was, says the historian Livy, the only foreign cult that Romulus adopted, the only foreign cult that lay within the *pomerium*, the sacred boundary of the city. It was the custom for traders to dedicate a tenth of their profit to Hercules, and victorious generals also made conspicuous donations. The income was not spent on grand buildings, and may have been devoted largely to the provision of a regular public feast, especially given that one of its rules was that all sacrificial meat, except that burned on the altars, was to be eaten on the premises.

We have several different versions of the legend associated with the Ara Maxima. All of them are substantially different from Virgil's, except for that of Ovid (*Fasti* V.541–586), which is itself based on Virgil. We can, therefore, see which features are likely to be Virgil's own and form an impression of the way he hoped the story would be understood.

At first Cacus seems to have been a benign figure of Roman legend. A path leading up from the Forum Boarium to the Palatine had the name *Scalae Caci* and somewhere in the vicinity of its foot was an *Atrium Caci*. He had a sister, Caca, for whom there seems to have existed a small shrine tended by the Vestal Virgins. But almost all those who tell his story represent him as a robber. It looks as if his name has been interpreted as the Greek work *kakos* – 'evil' (in spite of the difference between the long *a* of the Latin and the short *a* of the Greek). In this character he steals Hercules' cattle and conceals their destination by the trick of forcing them to walk backwards into his cave. Hercules does not notice the theft. He is asleep either through weariness or because he has been eating and drinking. On waking he notices the shortage. The missing cattle reveal their presence accidentally in one version and in another thanks to Hercules' stratagem in deliberately leading his remaining cattle past Cacus' cave door. Being found out, Cacus appeals to the locals for support against the foreigner, but is clubbed down and killed by Hercules. Evander, who recognises Hercules' future divinity because he has been informed by his prophetess-mother Carmentis, takes charge of the situation. In two of the prose versions it is he who establishes the altar, in one it is Hercules himself.

A version of the story appears in a poem by Virgil's contemporary Propertius in which Cacus has three bodies like Geryon. In the others Cacus is a mortal among mortals.

Virgil's Cacus is different. He is a son of Vulcan. He breathes fire and smoke. He is evidently of great and size and bulk. His cave is deep in the mountainside and is a place of horror, with the heads of his human victims nailed to its door. His theft of the cattle is no robbery for profit; it is done out of the sheer longing to do evil (205–6). He is a threat to all around.

Hercules has corresponding qualities. His arrival is described as 'the (miraculous) appearance of a god' (201). Insofar as to lose his cattle is to display human weakness, Virgil passes over it. Hercules does not stoop to a stratagem to track down the missing animals. He has challenged Cacus with their theft, but this only appears after the battle has been won (263). The focus is all on his search for a way into Cacus' cave, and the terrifying strength and determination he shows in finding it and destroying his foe. Compared with the other narratives, this is hyperbole on a huge scale.

What is Virgil's purpose in so emphasising the contest? A clear indication that it has become a battle on a superhuman level is given by the simile in 243–6: Cacus' home is like the realm of the dead, the pit of the underworld, which is alien to the gods above. Outside the simile, in the 'real world' it is the Giants, the traditional enemies of the gods, who are corralled in the Underworld. The giant Typhoeus, one of those who attempted to overthrow Jupiter, is traditionally confined below Mount Etna, where his fiery breath reaches the upper world through the eruptions of the volcano. Hercules' stupendous effort in dislodging the mountain crag that towers above Cacus' cave, along with his battering of Cacus with huge rocks, recall the rocks thrown by the gods and their opponents in Hesiod's *Theogony* ('Birth of the Gods'; Hesiod was a near-contemporary of Homer and almost equal to him in prestige). When Hercules hurls the rock the result (239–40) is a cosmic event involving the elements of sky (*aether*), earth (*ripae*) and water (*amnis*).

Seen thus, Cacus represents the forces of chaos and destruction that have threatened Aeneas before, in the storm-scene of Book I, and now in the events of Book VII, where we know that Juno and the Fury Allecto have been at work. It is not Aeneas who is threatened by Cacus, but Rome and the proto-Romans. Nevertheless, we and Aeneas may see Hercules' achievement as representing that which is Aeneas' own mission: the establishment of peace and order in the face of the forces of chaos. This is also Augustus' mission. Both Aeneas and Augustus are given Hercules-like characteristics, Aeneas in joining the company who have made the journey down to Hades and returned, and Augustus who even outdoes Hercules (VI.801–3). Scholars have also thought to see in Cacus a deliberate suggestion of Turnus as Aeneas' opponent and Antony as Augustus'.

The first reference to Hercules comes in 103, where he is referred to as *Amphitryoniades*, son of Amphitryon, his human father. At the end of the story, after our section ends, the Arcadians sing a hymn to Hercules, which concludes with a reference to his divine father (301): *Salve, vera Iovis proles, decus addite divis* (Hail, true son of Jupiter, yourself a glory given to the gods!). The story has been, among other things, an illustration of the principle *immortalitas virtute parta*, 'immortality achieved by excellence', Livy's phrase (I.7) for what inspired Romulus about Hercules. At the time when Virgil was composing the *Aeneid*, Horace was writing of Augustus (*Odes* III.3): 'By this quality (*sc.* that of being just and resolute) … Pollux and Hercules struggled for, and attained, the fiery citadels [of heaven]; and between them lies Augustus as he drinks the nectar with his bright-red lips.'

The principal non-Virgilian sources for the story of Hercules and Cacus are Livy I.7; Dionysius of Halicarnassus *Antiquitates Romanae* I.39–40; Diodorus of Sicily IV.21; and Propertius IV.9. Ovid *Fasti* I.541–586 is closely based on Virgil.

Further reading

There is no translation that is both worth reading in itself and a close guide to translation of the text. There are several on the internet that aim to perform the one or the other task. Of published texts, the ones that are probably most available are the Penguin translations by David West (1990) and Robert Fagles (2006). They are very different. West adopted a down-to-earth style that aims by sheer lucidity to convey Virgil's shades of meaning; Fagles uses (as indeed does Virgil) a more elevated style. Of older twentieth-century versions I find C. Day Lewis' the most interesting. More ambitious students may wish to look at John Dryden's version (1697), and if you are a Scot you should try your hand at Gavin Douglas' *Eneados* (1513) in the Scots tongue of that time; it is difficult but most rewarding.

There are several small and easily available introductions to Virgil and the *Aeneid*, which are eminently worth studying: W.A. Camps *An Introduction to Virgil* (OUP, 1969), Jasper Griffin *Virgil* (2nd edn Bristol Classical Press, 2001) and K.W. Gransden, updated by S.J. Harrison, *The Aeneid* (CUP, 2004).

Among editions of the whole of *Aeneid* VIII the most easily available are those by K.W. Gransden (Cambridge, 1976), C.J. Fordyce (Oxford, 1977) and R.D. Williams as part of his complete *Aeneid* (Bristol Classical Press, 1998).

Very useful works of reference are the *Oxford Classical Dictionary*, and Jenny March's *Dictionary of Classical Mythology* (Cassell, 1998).

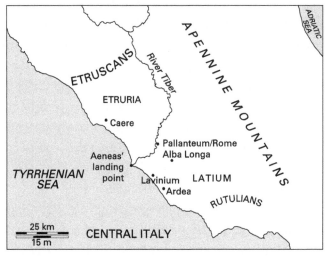

Map 1: Central Italy

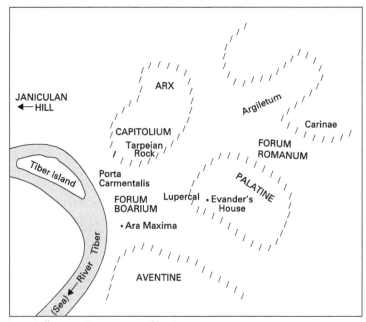

Map 2: Pallanteum/Rome as visited by Aeneas

Text

See Introduction pp. 26–7 for an explanation of the context.

Thybris ea fluvium, quam longa est, nocte tumentem
leniit, et tacita refluens ita substitit unda,
mitis ut in morem stagni placidaeque paludis
sterneret aequor aquis, remo ut luctamen abesset.
ergo iter inceptum celerant rumore secundo: 90
labitur uncta vadis abies; mirantur et undae,
miratur nemus insuetum fulgentia longe
scuta virum fluvio pictasque innare carinas.
olli remigio noctemque diemque fatigant
et longos superant flexus, variisque teguntur   95
arboribus, viridesque secant placido aequore silvas.
sol medium caeli conscenderat igneus orbem
cum muros arcemque procul ac rara domorum
tecta vident, quae nunc Romana potentia caelo
aequavit, tum res inopes Euandrus habebat.   100
ocius advertunt proras urbique propinquant.
    forte die sollemnem illo rex Arcas honorem
Amphitryoniadae magno divisque ferebat
ante urbem in luco. Pallas huic filius una,
una omnes iuvenum primi pauperque senatus   105
tura dabant, tepidusque cruor fumabat ad aras.
ut celsas videre rates atque inter opacum
adlabi nemus et tacitos incumbere remis,
terrentur visu subito cunctique relictis
consurgunt mensis. audax quos rumpere Pallas   110
sacra vetat raptoque volat telo obvius ipse,
et procul e tumulo: 'iuvenes, quae causa subegit
ignotas temptare vias? quo tenditis?' inquit.
'qui genus? unde domo? pacemne huc fertis an arma?'
tum pater Aeneas puppi sic fatur ab alta   115

paciferaeque manu ramum praetendit olivae:
'Troiugenas ac tela vides inimica Latinis,
quos illi bello profugos egere superbo.
Euandrum petimus. ferte haec et dicite lectos
Dardaniae venisse duces socia arma rogantes.'   120
obstipuit tanto percussus nomine Pallas:
'egredere o quicumque es' ait 'coramque parentem
adloquere ac nostris succede penatibus hospes.'
excepitque manu dextramque amplexus inhaesit;
progressi subeunt luco fluviumque relinquunt.   125
   tum regem Aeneas dictis adfatur amicis:
'optime Graiugenum, cui me Fortuna precari
et vitta comptos voluit praetendere ramos,
non equidem extimui Danaum quod ductor et Arcas
quodque a stirpe fores geminis coniunctus Atridis;   130
sed mea me virtus et sancta oracula divum
cognatique patres, tua terris didita fama,
coniunxere tibi et fatis egere volentem.
Dardanus, Iliacae primus pater urbis et auctor,
Electra, ut Grai perhibent, Atlantide cretus,   135
advehitur Teucros; Electram maximus Atlas
edidit, aetherios umero qui sustinet orbes.
vobis Mercurius pater est, quem candida Maia
Cyllenae gelido conceptum vertice fudit;
at Maiam, auditis si quicquam credimus, Atlas,   140
idem Atlas generat caeli qui sidera tollit.
sic genus amborum scindit se sanguine ab uno.
his fretus non legatos neque prima per artem
temptamenta tui pepigi; me, me ipse meumque
obieci caput et supplex ad limina veni.   145
gens eadem, quae te, crudeli Daunia bello
insequitur; nos si pellant, nihil afore credunt
quin omnem Hesperiam penitus sua sub iuga mittant,
et mare quod supra teneant quodque adluit infra.
accipe daque fidem. sunt nobis fortia bello   150

pectora, sunt animi et rebus spectata iuventus.'
    dixerat Aeneas. ille os oculosque loquentis
iamdudum et totum lustrabat lumine corpus.
tum sic pauca refert: 'ut te, fortissime Teucrum,
accipio agnoscoque lubens! ut verba parentis   155
et vocem Anchisae magni vultumque recordor!
nam memini Hesionae visentem regna sororis
Laomedontiaden Priamum Salamina petentem
protinus Arcadiae gelidos invisere fines.
tum mihi prima genas vestibat flore iuventas,   160
mirabarque duces Teucros, mirabar et ipsum
Laomedontiaden; sed cunctis altior ibat
Anchises. mihi mens iuvenali ardebat amore
compellare virum et dextrae coniungere dextram;
accessi et cupidus Phenei sub moenia duxi.   165
ille mihi insignem pharetram Lyciasque sagittas
discedens chlamydemque auro dedit intertextam,
frenaque bina meus quae nunc habet aurea Pallas.
ergo et quam petitis iuncta est mihi foedere dextra,
et lux cum primum terris se crastina reddet,   170
auxilio laetos dimittam opibusque iuvabo.
interea sacra haec, quando huc venistis amici,
annua, quae differre nefas, celebrate faventes
nobiscum, et iam nunc sociorum adsuescite mensis.'
    haec ubi dicta, dapes iubet et sublata reponi   175
pocula, gramineoque viros locat ipse sedili,
praecipuumque toro et villosi pelle leonis
accipit Aenean solioque invitat acerno.
tum lecti iuvenes certatim araeque sacerdos
viscera tosta ferunt taurorum, onerantque canistris   180
dona laboratae Cereris, Bacchumque ministrant.
vescitur Aeneas simul et Troiana iuventus
perpetui tergo bovis et lustralibus extis.
    postquam exempta fames et amor compressus edendi,
rex Euandrus ait: 'non haec sollemnia nobis,   185

has ex more dapes, hanc tanti numinis aram
vana superstitio veterumque ignara deorum
imposuit: saevis, hospes Troiane, periclis
servati facimus meritosque novamus honores.
iam primum saxis suspensam hanc aspice rupem,   190
disiectae procul ut moles desertaque montis
stat domus et scopuli ingentem traxere ruinam.
hic spelunca fuit vasto summota recessu,
semihominis Caci facies quam dira tenebat
solis inaccessam radiis; semperque recenti   195
caede tepebat humus, foribusque adfixa superbis
ora virum tristi pendebant pallida tabo.
huic monstro Volcanus erat pater: illius atros
ore vomens ignes magna se mole ferebat.
attulit et nobis aliquando optantibus aetas   200
auxilium adventumque dei. nam maximus ultor
tergemini nece Geryonae spoliisque superbus
Alcides aderat taurosque hac victor agebat
ingentes, vallemque boves amnemque tenebant.
at furis Caci mens effera, ne quid inausum   205
aut intractatum scelerisve dolive fuisset,
quattuor a stabulis praestanti corpore tauros
avertit, totidem forma superante iuvencas.
atque hos, ne qua forent pedibus vestigia rectis,
cauda in speluncam tractos versisque viarum   210
indiciis raptor saxo occultabat opaco;
quaerenti nulla ad speluncam signa ferebant.
interea, cum iam stabulis saturata moveret
Amphitryoniades armenta abitumque pararet,
discessu mugire boves atque omne querelis   215
impleri nemus et colles clamore relinqui.
reddidit una boum vocem, vastoque sub antro
mugiit, et Caci spem custodita fefellit.
hic vero Alcidae furiis exarserat atro
felle dolor: rapit arma manu nodisque gravatum   220

robur, et aërii cursu petit ardua montis.
tum primum nostri Cacum videre timentem
turbatumque oculis; fugit ilicet ocior Euro
speluncamque petit, pedibus timor addidit alas.
ut sese inclusit ruptisque immane catenis   225
deiecit saxum, ferro quod et arte paterna
pendebat, fultosque emuniit obice postes,
ecce furens animis aderat Tirynthius, omnemque
accessum lustrans huc ora ferebat et illuc,
dentibus infrendens. ter totum fervidus ira   230
lustrat Aventini montem, ter saxea temptat
limina nequiquam, ter fessus valle resedit.
stabat acuta silex praecisis undique saxis
speluncae dorso insurgens, altissima visu,
dirarum nidis domus opportuna volucrum.   235
hanc, ut prona iugo laevum incumbebat ad amnem,
dexter in adversum nitens concussit et imis
avulsam solvit radicibus, inde repente
impulit; impulsu quo maximus intonat aether,
dissultant ripae refluitque exterritus amnis.   240
at specus et Caci detecta apparuit ingens
regia, et umbrosae penitus patuere cavernae,
non secus ac si qua penitus vi terra dehiscens
infernas reseret sedes et regna recludat
pallida, dis invisa, superque immane barathrum   245
cernatur, trepident immisso lumine Manes.
ergo insperata deprensum luce repente
inclusumque cavo saxo atque insueta rudentem
desuper Alcides telis premit, omniaque arma
advocat et ramis vastisque molaribus instat.   250
ille autem, neque enim fuga iam super ulla pericli,
faucibus ingentem fumum (mirabile dictu)
evomit involvitque domum caligine caeca
prospectum eripiens oculis, glomeratque sub antro
fumiferam noctem commixtis igne tenebris.   255

non tulit Alcides animis, seque ipse per ignem
praecipiti iecit saltu, qua plurimus undam
fumus agit nebulaque ingens specus aestuat atra.
hic Cacum in tenebris incendia vana vomentem
corripit in nodum complexus, et angit inhaerens   260
elisos oculos et siccum sanguine guttur.
panditur extemplo foribus domus atra revulsis
abstractaeque boves abiurataeque rapinae
caelo ostenduntur, pedibusque informe cadaver
protrahitur. nequeunt expleri corda tuendo   265
terribiles oculos, vultum villosaque saetis
pectora semiferi atque exstinctos faucibus ignes.
ex illo celebratus honos laetique minores
servavere diem, primusque Potitius auctor
et domus Herculei custos Pinaria sacri   270
hanc aram luco statuit, quae maxima semper
dicetur nobis et erit quae maxima semper.
quare agite, o iuvenes, tantarum in munere laudum
cingite fronde comas et pocula porgite dextris.
communemque vocate deum et date vina volentes.'   275
dixerat, Herculea bicolor cum populus umbra
velavitque comas foliisque innexa pependit,
et sacer implevit dextram scyphus. ocius omnes
in mensam laeti libant divosque precantur.

For a summary of lines 280–557, see the section on Book VIII, pp. 28–30

tum pater Euandrus dextram complexus euntis
haeret inexpletus lacrimans ac talia fatur:
'o mihi praeteritos referat si Iuppiter annos,   560
qualis eram cum primam aciem Praeneste sub ipsa
stravi scutorumque incendi victor acervos
et regem hac Erulum dextra sub Tartara misi,
nascenti cui tres animas Feronia mater
(horrendum dictu) dederat, terna arma movenda –   565

ter leto sternendus erat; cui nunc tamen omnes
abstulit haec animas dextra et totidem exuit armis:
non ego nunc dulci amplexu divellerer usquam,
nate, tuo, neque finitimo Mezentius umquam
huic capiti insultans tot ferro saeva dedisset 570
funera, tam multis viduasset civibus urbem.
at vos, o superi, et divum tu maxime rector
Iuppiter, Arcadii, quaeso, miserescite regis
et patrias audite preces. si numina vestra
incolumem Pallanta mihi, si fata reservant, 575
si visurus eum vivo et venturus in unum,
vitam oro, patior quemvis durare laborem.
sin aliquem infandum casum, Fortuna, minaris,
nunc, nunc o liceat crudelem abrumpere vitam,
dum curae ambiguae, dum spes incerta futuri, 580
dum te, care puer, mea sola et sera voluptas,
complexu teneo, gravior neu nuntius aures
vulneret. haec genitor digressu dicta supremo
fundebat; famuli conlapsum in tecta ferebant.

Commentary Notes

Grammatical references in these Notes are to the New Latin Grammar (NLG) of Project Gutenberg, available at www.gutenberg.org/ebooks/15665

Terms marked with an asterisk are explained in the glossary section included in the Introduction, pp. 17–20.

For the content of 1–85, see the Section on Book VIII, pp. 26–7.

86–101

The river-god ensures an easy passage for Aeneas and his men. They have a pleasant journey up to Pallanteum, where we have the first of many comparisons with the simplicity of Evander's city and the magnificence of Augustus'.

86–9 'That night [i.e. the one following the sacrifice] – during the whole length of it – Tiber calmed his swollen stream, and, holding-his-current-back (*refluens*) was so still with [his] silent water, that he laid a flat surface (*aequor*) upon the waters, so that there should be no effort for the oar.' This is the generally accepted version of this passage. See companion website for some different observations.

86 Thybris: Virgil's most frequently used word for the river (otherwise *Tiberis, Tiberinus*). With its long first syllable it can stand at the head of a line.

est: this present tense has always seemed slightly odd. 'Historic present' is suggested, although it is not quite like the normal 'historic' present, which is used to bring individual elements of a narrative vividly before the reader's eyes (three such verbs in 90–91).

quam longa: a sort of shortened version of *quam longa est, tam diu tumebat* …, … 'for as long as the night (lasted), so long did (the river) flow high' (cf. *Aen*.IV.193).

87   refluens: the word appears twice elsewhere in the *Aeneid*: (i) VIII.240, where the river *flows backwards* (in terror), and (ii) IX.33, where the Nile flood subsides and the waters *flow back down* into their normal channel. West translates with a strong version of (i): 'reversing his current', but the point here is the transition from the swollen (*tumentem*) river in spate to the placid still waters, so something more like meaning (ii) seems indicated. *substitit* 'came to a halt' seems to support this. *ita* looks forward to *ut*: 'came to such a complete stop that . . . . . .'.

88–9   in morem + gen.: 'like' (for the acc. see OLD *in* 18). *stagnum* and *palus* regularly of standing water, often left-over flood water, but without the slightly noxious implications of 'stagnant' or 'swamp'. *-que* is more like 'or' here than 'and'. *aequor* regularly means 'a flat surface', without itself containing the idea of 'water'. Notice the complicated alliteration* of these two lines.

89   remo ut luctamen abesset: 'so that strain should be absent from the oar', i.e. 'so that the oarsmen should feel no strain'. (*luctamen* is based on the verb *luctor*, which conveys the idea of competitive struggle, here competition against an opposing current.) This is a purpose clause dependent on *sterneret*, which itself is part of the result clause introduced by *ita*. . . . . *ut*. *remo* is abl. of separation (NLG 214).

90   rumore secundo: *secundus* is an old participle of *sequor* (so 'following', hence 'favourable' of the wind in a ship's sails). Virgil seems to be quoting Ennius *Annals*: *populi rumore secundo* (*Ann*. 255V), where the meaning is clearly 'with accompanying sounds of support', i.e. cheers from those on the bank (cf. V.338 *fremitu secundo*, 491 *clamore secundo*).

91   abies: fir-wood, metonymy* for 'the ship'. *uncta*: hulls were smeared with wax or pitch as a preservative. *ungere* can also make something slippery, so the word adds to the idea of smooth passage. *vădis*: (abl. of place, found without a proposition regularly in verse) originally 'shallows', 'water to walk through (*vādo* – the long 'a' appears in Eng. 'wade')' later used of waters in general.

91–3.   mirantur ... miratur: the anaphora* connects the two sentences of which these are the verbs, and also emphasises the idea of 'wonder'. Take *et* ('even') with both, as *insuetum*, though agreeing only with *nemus*, will apply also to *undae*, both personified*. 'The very waters gaze in amazement, as does the forest, unfamiliar as it is (to the sight of such things), at the warriors' shields glinting far off over the stream and (are astonished that) that there are painted hulls afloat on it.' Take *scuta* as dir. obj. of *mirantur/miratur*; then there is a slight change of construction as *mirantur* now introduces an acc. and infin. ('they are astonished that . . .') *carinas innare. Fluvio* can be understood with both *fulgentia* and *innare*. (If with *innare*, note that *-que* is delayed; grammatically, one would expect *fluvioque*.)

virum (old form of gen.pl.) must suggest something more positive than simply 'men': hence 'warriors'.

94–6   The four main verbs of these lines, with their unremarkable connectors *et*, *-que*, *-que*, create the impression of a very ordered and unhurried journey. Looked at in a literal way, the Trojans are travelling some 30km (Googlemap directions) in the greater part of twenty-four hours, which, given the lack of adverse current (87), should require no special effort. (The Wikipedia article on 'Galley' is well-documented.) The charm of their surroundings (woods and long reaches of water) creates a double contrast: (i) with the Tiber in Virgil's own day ('distinctly industrial, beset with warehouses, jetties, and dumps' – Andrew Wallace-Hadrill, in an email), and (ii) between this scene and the fearful war towards which it is working. **olli**: dat. of archaic* form of **ille**. **-que . . . -que**: 'both . . . and'. **remigio**: instrumental abl. **superant**: 'they go past'. **variis**: 'all manner of'.

97   medium caeli . . . orbem: 'the middle of the arch of heaven'.

98   procul: the *u* is short by nature but, coming first in its foot, takes the place of a long syllable. The feature, *'brevis in longo'*, occurs fifty-seven times in Virgil and always at a word-ending. It creates a deliberately uncomfortable hold-up of the rhythm (Virgil could have avoided it by writing, e.g. *tum* instead of *ac*) for which the only general explanation appears to be conscious archaism* – recalling the style of Ennius (compare *olli* in 94 and Intro p. 7.)

99   vident: for the indic. see NLG288.2 'Cum Inversum'. It means nearly 'And then . . .' The historic present is more striking for its context of pluperf., perf., imperf.

quae: grammatically in agreement only with n.pl. *tecta*, but actually referring to all three elements of what can be seen of Pallanteum. *caelo aequavit*: a striking enjambment*, drawing attention to the hyperbole*, and pointing to the great contrast between the *nunc* of Virgil's day and the *tum* of Evander's.

100   res inopes: in apposition to *quae*. 'Which at that time Evander owned as his impoverished possessions.'

101   ocius: the comparative form used not in a comparison but to suggest 'pretty quickly'. It gives a sense of urgency. *urbi*: Virgil refers to Pallanteum as *urbs* in two other places in VIII, but here especially it seems to create a contrast between present insignificance and future glory (cf. 99).

102–125

The Arcadians are alarmed at the sight of warships approaching, but Evander's son Pallas quickly makes friendly contact with Aeneas.

102 rex Arcas: the Arcadian king, i.e. Evander. *sollemnem:* 'due' (see vocab.) in the sense that it was a regular event.

103 Amphitryoniadae: dat.: the son of Amphitryon, Hercules (*-ides* and *-ades* are Greek suffixes meaning 'son of': cf. 158; such words are 'patronymics'). Strictly, Hercules was Jupiter's son; Amphitryon was his mother Alcmene's husband.

104 ante urbem: The altar of Hercules (Ara Maxima) known to Virgil was in the Forum Boarium ('Cattle Market') on the banks of the Tiber on the flat ground between the Capitol, the Palatine and the Aventine, just where ships coming upriver would moor (Map p. 36).

huic: rather than take this with *una* (the normal expression is *una cum*), we should probably understand *erat*, and *huic* as dat. of possession: 'His son Pallas (was) with him'. *una. . . una:* the repetition emphasises that the community was as one in this celebration.

105 omnes iuvenum primi: *primi* as a noun 'the first ones', 'leaders'; *iuvenum* partitive gen.: 'the first among the young men'.

106 ad aras: *ad* can often mean 'near' and occasionally almost 'on' (OLD 13, 15). Blood would be poured on the altar as part of the ritual of sacrifice, but it would also fall on the ground. *fumabat:* 'was steaming' because the sacrificial victims had only very recently been killed. The plural 'altars' suggests the sacrifice of several animals; at the same time the simple offering of incense (*tura*) is consistent with the poverty of the community. (In *Odes* IV.2.49–52 Horace suggests that an offering of *tus* is something that every citizen can manage.) Virgil telescopes events of the ceremony: in 106 the participants are offering incense, in 110 they are all seated at table.

107–8 vīdēre for vīdērunt ('syncopated perfect'): 'When they saw the lofty ships, and that they were slipping nearer through the shadowy wood and that (their crews) were working hard at their oars in silence ...': *rates* starts as the obj. of *videre*, then becomes the (acc.) subj. of *adlabi*, then *tacitos* ('silent men') takes over as subj. of *incumbere*. This is how West takes it; one could also have *tacitos* as the subj. of both infinitives. The first version seems to offer the best preparation for *terrentur*: the ships emerge from the darkness under the trees; they move softly nearer; their oarsmen are working in silence (which Servius explains as 'with no timing call being given'). It all looks like a surprise attack.

110–11 quos: connecting relative 'and them'; it is postponed to emphasise *audax*. 'And without a thought, Pallas told them not to interrupt the sacrifice ...'. The adj. ('ready to dare', 'prepared to do something without worrying about the consequences') refers to a quality that can be attractive, but is also dangerous. (*vetat, rapto telo, volat* and *obvius* all contribute to this impression.)

rumpere . . . sacra: if a ritual procedure were flawed or interrupted it would have to be repeated from the beginning. (The process is called *instauratio*.)

111 rapto . . . telo: abl. abs. *ipse*: 'on his own'.

114 qui genus: sc. *estis? genus* is 'acc. of respect': 'Who are you (as regards) race?' **unde domo**: an idiomatic abbreviation of 'Where is the home you come from? **arma**: to be understood as a metonymy* for 'war', since 'arms' are already visible: shields (93) and the *tela*, which Aeneas is about to acknowledge (117). Servius' comment is that these quick-fire urgent questions are harassing.

115 **pater Aeneas**: 18 times in the *Aeneid*. *Pater Anchises* 17 times, of 7 others, once each: a distinct mark of respect. **puppi . . . ab alta**: a line curiously like II.2: *inde toro pater Aeneas sic orsus ab alto.*

116 **paciferae . . . olivae**: a traditional method of showing that you come in peace.

117 'We are Trojans. The weapons you see are directed against the Latins.' As Servius observes, a useful argument in view of the advice given by the river god in VIII.55: '(The Arcadians) are at constant war with the Latins.' Take *Latinis* closely with *inimica.*

118 **quos** referring to the Trojans, *illi* to the Latins. *ēgēre* = *ēgērunt* (syncopated perf. as in 107). The sentence: either (i) 'whom they have driven out in presumptuous war, (although they are) refugees' or (ii) 'whom they have driven into exile (*profugos* proleptic* NLG 374.5) in . . . war'. With the simple verb *egere*, (ii) is probably preferable. It contributes more to what is anyway a distinctly partial version of the events of Book VII. In it fighting begins not, as Aeneas suggests here, because of the contemptuous arrogance of the Latini, but as the result of an accident. Day Lewis translates: 'Who have driven us out of their land by a cynical act of aggression.' *superbo* is a transferred epithet*, describing the Latini, not the war.

119 **Evandrum petimus**: Aeneas has cleared up misunderstandings. He now makes a very short and simple statement of his mission. **ferte**: pl; evidently some of the Arcadians have come to Pallas' support since 111.

120 **Dardaniae**: Dardania is the land of Troy, taking its name from its forefather Dardanus. The name takes rhetorical emphasis from its place in the line. *socia arma*: 'an army in alliance'.

121 Pallas' reaction is very strong, given by both *obstipuit* and *percussus*. **nomine**: i.e. that of Dardanus, whose importance appears from Aeneas' forthcoming speech.

122-3   egredere: imperative (2nd sing) of *egredior*. After a shaky start (114) disembarkation and welcome proceed rapidly, to the extent that Aeneas never introduces himself by name. **o quicumque es**: It intensifies the feeling behind *o* to place it after the verb expressing the wish (religious language: 4.578, 8.27). **coram** is an adverb: 'speak to my father face to face'. **adloquere**: imperative as *egredere*. **penatibus**: the *penates* are the household gods, so come to represent, and thus to mean 'home'; the dat. ('of direction' NLG 193) is quite common with *succedo* meaning 'to come into an appropriate place'. **hospes**: 'as a guest', i.e. Aeneas' answer has fully satisfied Pallas.

124   Pallas' warm welcome is expressed in two separate phrases. **dextram amplexus**: he grasps Aeneas' hand in both his own.

125   luco: dat. of direction as with *succede* 123.

126-151

Aeneas introduces himself. He is confident of a kindly reception (127-133); he and Evander have a common ancestor in Atlas (133-142); the Trojans need Evander's help, as Evander needs the Trojans' (143-151).

127   Graiugenum: archaic* form of the gen. pl. **optime Gr.** as *iuvenum primi* 105 – partitive gen. **cui**: the person to whom prayers are addressed is everywhere else (OLD) in the acc. Possibly the dat. is justified here by the fact the word does not mean 'to pray *for* something', but, so far, simply 'to utter a prayer'.

128   voluit: 'decided' (suggested by the perf. – 'a single act of wishing'); cf. Caesar's *hoc voluerunt* – 'It was their decision' (Suetonius *Julius* 30.4) of his opponents at Pharsalus. **vitta comptos ramos**: 'branches dressed with bands of wool'. This seems a slight extension of the idea of *paciferae olivae* (116) into the ceremonial required for a formal supplication, for which *precari* and *supplex* (145) are appropriate – see companion website note on 145.

129 **Read:** *non extimui quod fores ductor Danaum et Arcas* … : *Danaum* is gen.pl. **fores** = *esses*, from the same tense as the standard *foret* and *forent*. It is subjunctive because of an implied indirect quality (NLG 323) in the clause 'because of the idea that you were …' – an idea that is obliterated or contradicted by the emphatic indicative *coniunxere* of 133. *Arcas*: Arcadian therefore *Greek*.

130 **a stirpe:** from your origin. **Atridis:** *Atridae*, spelled *Atreidae* in Greek, a patronymic (103): 'sons of Atreus'. That is: Agamemnon (commander of the Greeks at Troy) and Menelaus (husband of Helen). In spite of efforts, even Servius strained to find a convincing family relationship between Evander and the Atridae: it was either a marriage relationship through Leda, Agamemnon's mother-in-law, or a blood relationship stretching back to Atlas!

131–3 'My quality, the holy oracles, our kindred fathers, your renowned name – all have brought me here by destiny (and) glad (at it).' *me* is obj. of *coniunxere* and *egere* in 133 (both syncopated perf.). The self-confidence is underlined by the polyptoton* *mea me*. *oracula*: this refers most obviously to the Sibyl's prophecy (VI.96–7: see the Summary) and Tiberinus' instructions (VIII.51–8: see note before 86). **cognatique patres:** '(The fact that our) fathers (were) related'. The four phrases of these two lines have a variety of connexions: *et*, *-que* and the contrasting initial words *mea* and *tua*. **tua … fama** is mere diplomatic politeness: Aeneas had not even heard of Evander until two nights before. **terris:** abl. of place closely with *didita* 'spread widely'.

134–142 Aeneas' argument: We are your kith and kin; we have the same enemies; we shall be reliable allies. **Iliacae … auctor:** Dardanus was a forefather more than a founder: his own city was Dardania; Troy was built by his great-grandson Ilus. The genealogy to which Aeneas is referring can be set out like this:

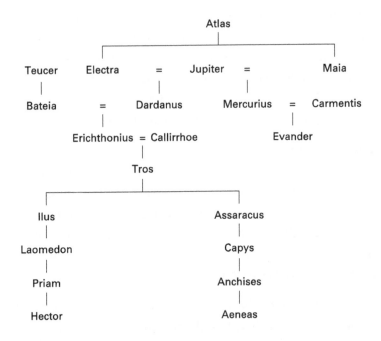

Aeneas could have made a much simpler common ancestry if he had referred to his mother Venus, daughter of Jupiter as Mercury was his son, thus revealing himself and Dardanus as first cousins. Plainly, one reason for his not doing so is that this would exclude the whole Trojan line, which needs to be part of the story.

135   cretus is past part. of *cresco* as if the verb were transitive; translate 'having been grown', 'originating'. **Electra**: abl. of source (NLG 215) 'from'.

136–41   Teucros: acc. governed by the *ad* in *advehitur* (VII.216 *urbem adferimur*). The *Teucri* are the people of Teucer (genealogy above). Virgil's version of the story (VII.205–11) is that Dardanus came from his home Corythus in Italy to Asia Minor and married Teucer's daughter. Atlas is the giant who holds the heavens up on his shoulders.

vobis: 'pater', of Mercury, is literally true for Evander; for others *pater* has the same sort of meaning as *pater Aeneas* (115). **candida**: because she is beautiful, also because she is 'shining', as a star, one of the Pleiades. **Cyllene** is an impressive mountain in the northern Peloponnese, Mercury's legendary birth-place. **gelido vertice** seems to go with both *conceptum* and *fudit* 'gave birth to'.

at: introduces the punch line (OLD3 'but lo and behold'); then *generat* can be thought of as historic present, in narrative contrast with perf. *fudit*. **quicquam**: adverbial 'in any way'.

142   amborum: 'of both (you and me)'. **scindit se**: 'separates itself', 'divides' (intrans.).

143–4   his … pepigi: A somewhat tangled sentence, reflecting Aeneas' agitation. *Pango* is a formal word and goes naturally with nouns like *foedus* and means 'establish, set up (a treaty)'. But all Aeneas has 'set up' is the chance to make 'a trial' of Evander. If *temptamenta* (here only in Virgil) sounds forced as an object of *pepigi, legatos* sounds more so. Williams translates 'Putting my trust in this I did not send envoys or arrange my first approaches to you by diplomacy (*per artem*)', understanding out of *pepigi* another verb ('send') to govern *legatos*.

tui is gen. of the pronoun *tu*, rarely used because 'of you' (possessive) is usually done with the adjective *tuus*. Here the gen. is not possessive but 'objective', as in the phrase *amor patriae* 'love of one's country', here 'trials of you' (NLG 242.2).

144–5   meum caput 'my own person' (*caput* OLD 3,4 or 7) is barely distinguishable from (repeated) 'me', thus further intensifying the urgent emphasis. **obieci**: 'I have put my own person in the way (of danger)'. **supplex veni**: 'I have come as a suppliant'. To be a suppliant is to throw oneself on someone's mercy.

146 'The same nation is harassing us which (is harassing) you, (that is) the Daunian nation, in a brutal war.' (*Insequitur* must be understood in both the main clause and the relative clause.) In the standard geography of ancient Italy Daunia refers to an area of Apulia, in the heel of Italy, of which a Daunus was mythical king (Hor. *Odes* III.30.11). Here 'Daunian' derives from a different Daunus, Turnus' father, king of the Rutuli, whose home is at Ardea, some 30km down the coast from the Tiber estuary.

147–8 **nihil afore .... quin mittant**: 'They think there will be nothing missing (*afore* fut. infin. of *absum*) so that they do not bring...' i.e. 'They think there will be nothing to stop them bringing ...'. The 'yoke' metaphor* is familiar from Greek literature, but we should also think of *mittere sub iugum*, a phrase that refers to the process of unconditional surrender in the military terms of later Roman history – 'to send under the yoke'.

149 Translate *quin ... mittant et teneant mare quod supra adluit quodque infra adluit*. The Adriatic 'washes (the coast) above' and the Tyrrhenian sea that below. (See map p.36.)

Aeneas' appeal in lines 146–9 is of very doubtful justification. Evander's own quarrel is with the Latins (55). Turnus and the Daunians have only been brought into the matter because of the offence taken by Turnus, and caused by Aeneas, over Lavinia. To exaggerate the threat presented by your own opponent in order to bring another party into the conflict is a traditional diplomatic trick.

150 **fidem**: 'promise'.

151 **rebus spectata**: 'proved by experience', *res* covering all that had happened to the Trojans. **nobis**: possessive dat. – 'we have hearts ...' **bello** (with *fortia*): either dat. 'brave for war' or abl. 'brave in war'.

152-174

Evander's response. He remembers an event of long ago when Aeneas' own father Anchises accompanied Priam on a visit to Evander's native Arcadia; Evander had been captivated by Anchises and a guest friendship established between their families by gifts. He now invites Aeneas and his company to join the feast.

151-2 **dixerat:** the pluperf. gives the firm sense 'he had finished'. **ille:** i.e. Evander. **lustrabat:** *lustro* originally 'to go round as a ritual', hence, 'to purify' and (rather differently, as here) 'to gaze at'. Take *iamdudum* closely with it: 'for some time now'.

154 **pauca:** Evander's speech is not especially short, but Romans prided themselves on being laconic, and this is a word of approval for a sensible speech by a good person. **ut** here with *libens* = 'how gladly!' (Vocab. under (3): as also 155.) **Teucrum:** gen. pl.

155-6 **parentis ... Anchisae:** '*your* father Anchises'. In one way or another, Anchises plays a crucial part in *Aeneid* I-VI. (See online Summary under these books.)

157-9 Evander remembers Priam, King of Troy visiting Greece to see his sister Hesione who was living in Salamis. Take the sentence: *memini Priamum, visentem regna sororis, Salamina* (acc. sing.) *petentem, protinus Arcadiae fines invisere.* 'I remember that Priam, visiting his sister's kingdom, making for Salamis, went straight on to visit ...'. The two participles *visentem* and *petentem* make for an awkward sentence where it isn't clear what was the sequence of destinations in the travels of Priam, king of Troy: Arcadia first or second? Is the awkwardness in Evander's memory? **protinus:** 'straight on'. **invisere:** one might expect a perf. infin., but after *memini* Virgil much prefers the vividness of the present. **Salamina:** (Greek) acc. of *Salamis*, the island off Athens' coastline, an independent city-state until the sixth century BCE.

158 Laomedontiaden: Greek acc. of the patronymic (103n.) *Laomedontiades*, son of Laomedon, i.e. Priam.

159 gelidos: Arcadia is a high plateau with higher peaks and, therefore, conventionally chilly.

160 mihi: so-called dat. of reference (NLG 188). 'As for me, earliest youth covered . . .', but it can be translated as 'my cheeks'. **vestibat:** an archaic* version of the standard but unscannable *vestiebat*. In *Il.*XXIV.348 and *Od.*X.279 Hermes/Mercury presents himself as 'a young man with his first beard growing – the most attractive age.'

161–3 et: either delayed 'and I admired' or emphatic with *ipsum*. There are three clauses here, each ending with an object of Evander's admiration, each more emphatic than its predecessor. The switch from *mirabar* to *sed . . . ibat* also serves to intensify Evander's feelings, as does the fact that *Teucros* and *Laomedontiaden* are acc., while *Anchises* is nom. and subject.

162 cunctis altior ibat: 'stepped out taller than all'. For the Romans the way one walked was an indicator of character.

163–4 'My mind was on fire with a young man's eagerness to address the great man.' *amore*: the noun can introduce the infinitive, being related to a verb upon which an infinitive could naturally depend. *virum*: again a term of positive respect (93). *ardebat amore*: alliteration* suggesting strong feeling.

165 Phĕnĕī : Why Pheneus? It is a long way from Evander's Arcadian Pallantion. In one version (though not Virgil's, see 136–41n.) it was Dardanus' birthplace. Also, it is just under Mount Cyllene, where the principal temple was to Hermes/Mercury, Evander's father.

167 intertextam: note the rare verse-end with two spondees.

168   Read *frenaque bina aurea, quae Pallas meus nunc habet. bina*:
strictly a 'distributive' numeral – 'two each', but used instead of *duo*
with nouns that have a plural but not a singular, as is almost entirely
true of *frena* (see OLD).

169–70   'And so as far as I am concerned, first, the right hand (of
friendship) which you are seeking has been united (to yours) by
a solemn agreement, and, second . . .'. *dextra* is strikingly delayed until
the end of the sentence. Emphatic *et . . . et* translated as 'first' and
second'.

dextram iungere: to join hands, i.e. to make a pledge. (i) It is possible
that the *foedus* is constituted by the handshake now given by Evander
to Aeneas and is an answer to 150 *accipe daque fidem*. In that case
mihi (untranslated above) is dat. of agent (NLG 189) 'by me'. (ii) Also
possible, and perhaps more likely: the *foedus* is the relationship of
amicitia and *hospitium* ('guest-friendship') established between
Anchises and Evander long ago. In that case *mihi* should be translated
'as far as I am concerned' (dat. of reference NLG 188). Taken this way,
the old strength of feeling that Evander describes (161–5) now finds
its outlet in the idea '(you do not need to ask:) the pledge . . . has
already been made.'

170   *crastina* grammatically with *lux*, but having the sense of adv. –
cras, ubi lux se reddet; the reflexive *se reddet* is indistinguishable from
redibit.

171   **auxilio**: military forces; *opibus*: supplies; instrumental abl.
(NLG 218).

172–4   Read *haec annua sacra celebrate quae nefas (est) differre.*
quando here = 'since', not 'when'. **amici**: 'as friends'. **faventes**:
'wholeheartedly'. **adsuescite**: 'grow accustomed to' (*mensis* is dat.),
trans. 'make yourselves familiar with'.

175–183

The feast is resumed. Aeneas is given the place of honour.

175   haec ubi dicta: understand *dedit* (the expression used 8 times in *Aen.*) or *sunt*. **sublata**: 'removed' should be understood with *dapes* as well as with *pocula*. In spite of Pallas' appeal (110–111 and cf. the note there about restarting rituals) some interruption has taken place.

176   sedili (abl. of place): The ancient commentator Macrobius noted (III.6.16) that 'at festivals of Hercules it is correct practice to sit while eating' – as opposed to the normal practice of lying on couches. So also *solio* (178). The *gramineum sedile* is presumably a bench made of turf. **ipse**: i.e. being the attentive host, not leaving it to his assistants.

177   praecipuum: 'as his most important (guest)' – as his place in the line shows – OLD3b. **toro**: a *torus* (OLD4a) is a cushion or other soft covering for a hard chair or couch: here 'a lion skin covering' making *toro et . . . pelle* a hendiadys*.

178   Aenean: Greek acc. **invitat**: 'entertain' here (OLD1) rather than 'invite', so *solio* is abl. of place.

180   viscera: 'everything under the hide' (Servius on I.211). **onerant**: 'they load (bread) into baskets (*canistris* dat. of indirect object)'; for the other construction X.868: *manus iaculis oneravit*: 'he loaded his hands with spears'.

181   Cereris, Bacchum: metonymy* for bread and wine; *laboratae* 'well-worked' applied to Ceres as if there were no personification*.

183   perpetui tergo bovis: an oddly transferred epithet* – the adjective 'full-length' belongs to *tergo*. 'The full-length chine' (= meat off the backbone) is a reference to Homeric meals: in *Od.* XIV.437 it is a special cut reserved for Odysseus. **lustralibus** would naturally suggest an association with purification (see note on 153), but there seems to be none here. Fordyce suggests 'sacrificial, in a general sense'. **extis:** abl. regular after *vescor* 'feed on'.

184–279

Evander tells how some of Hercules' cattle were stolen by the giant Cacus and how Hercules killed Cacus in revenge.

184–199 Cacus and his cave.

On Hercules and the Ara Maxima, see Introduction pp. 30–34.

The story serves at least three purposes: (i) Evander's explanation to the Trojans of what is happening, (188, 190); (ii) a sermon by Evander addressed to his own people as well as the Trojans, encouraging their devotion to Hercules (273); and (iii) Virgil's narrative directed to his readers, offering a dramatic tale and an aetiological account of the Ara Maxima celebrations (269–272). At one point at least (see 268 note) the simultaneous presence of elements (ii) and (iii) causes slight confusion.

184 Read *postquam fames exempta est et amor edendi compressus est.*

185–9 Read *non vana superstitio . . . imposuit haec sollemnia . . . .* '(It was) not an *empty* superstition nor one (which is) *unaware* of the old gods (which) *imposed* these rites'. **ex more dapes:** 'a feast celebrated in the traditional way', i.e. properly, decently. **tanti numinis:** either (i) possessive gen.: 'this altar belonging to so great a god' (*numen* = 'god', i.e. Hercules (OLD6)), or (ii) gen. of quality (NLG 203): 'this altar with such divinity about it' (*numen* = 'divine majesty' (OLD4)).

imposuit: *non* in 185 covers this word too: 'it was not a matter of having things imposed on us: we were glad to ...'; and *saevis*, emphasised by its separation from *periclis*, gives the reason. **facimus**: best to take this as OLD24b does: 'perform sacrifice'. The two points are then separate: 'we sacrifice because we have been rescued, and the honours we repeat (or 'institute' – see following note) are well-earned.'

novamus: (i) we repeat from year to year (OLD7); (ii) we institute as new (OLD1). Usage seems to favour (i) – cf. the references in OLD. In fact the ceremony has been going on for some years already (173, 185), hence, 'we repeat'. But there is an element of self-justification in what Evander says, and what he is justifying (to Aeneas, and to Aeneas' Roman descendants) is the institution of a novel cult. This comes out much more clearly with (ii). 'We are in the process of instituting a cult', which cannot be secure until performed over many years – hence the present tense.

190-2 iam primum: an introductory phrase to Evander's story. He is pointing to the Aventine Hill (plan, p. 36). (The spondaic line 190 makes for a slow, portentous introduction.) Evander's description is difficult to disentangle in detail, though the gist is clear. Here is a suggestion. *suspensam* 'vaulted' is an architect's term (OLD4c). 'See that cliff (like) a vault (built out) of rocks [*saxis* abl. of the material out of which something is made: 7.639]: how (*ut*: vocab (3)) the masses have been hurled far apart (from each other) [understand *sunt* with *disiectae*], and the mountain-house stands abandoned and the crags have brought down immense destruction.' [*traxēre* for *traxērunt*]

193 vasto summota recessu: 'stretching away with a vast distance back'; the abl. is 'attendant circumstance' (NLG 221). *recessu* in itself adds nothing to *summota*, but admits an additional idea in the adj. *vasto*, which conveys the sense 'huge, desolate and frightening'.

194 'Which the hideous appearance of the half-human Cacus occupied'. *Facies* is an abstract noun – 'appearance' is the root meaning of *facies* (OLD1); 'face' is derivative (OLD9). *semihominis*: scan — ˘˘ —. *-miho-* is run together as a single short syllable '-myo-' ('synizesis'). *Caci*: his name 'the evil one' (by taking the Greek word and lengthening its first syllable) is a conscious contrast to Evander's: 'the good man' in Greek.

195 solis inaccessam radiis: 'inaccessible to sunlight'. The darkness of Cacus' cave here prepares us for the flood of light in 241–247.

197 pallida: either closely with *tabo*: 'discoloured with horrid decay', or *tristi tabo* is abl. of description (NLG 224) 'pale faces in a state of horrid decay'.

198 huic monstro: possessive dat. **illius**: i.e. Vulcan's. On Cacus' origins see Introduction, p. 32. Vulcan will play a very different role in VIII.370–453, when, at Venus' request, he makes the armour for Aeneas which is the focus of attention for the last 120 lines of the book.

198–9 atros. . .ignes: 'dark fires', an expression containing contradictory ideas – 'oxymoron'. Dido used the phrase at *Aen.*IV.384 'I shall pursue you with dark fires'. It is a vivid and sinister expression; here more concretely intelligible of smoke and flame, but still forceful. **magna . . . ferebat**: *mole* is 'abl. of manner' (NLG 220); it can be translated as adv.: 'he moved heavily along'; 'he hauled his lumbering hulk' (Fagles). '*Se ferre* is used to imply an impressive carriage' (Fordyce).

200–279

Hercules comes to the rescue. His Tenth Labour was to steal the cattle of Geryon, the three-bodied giant who lived in the farthest west.

Having killed Geryon he had to get the cattle back to Argos, and came via the future site of Rome.

200-1 'Even to us longing for it time in the end brought the arrival and assistance of a god' – i.e. 'brought a god to appear and save us.' *et nobis*: 'even to us'. *aliquando*: 'at long last'. *optantibus* does not suggest prayer (to which one hopes for an answer) but simple delight when a good thing happens – the Arcadians had not seen *any* way out of their predicament. *aetas*: 'time' not 'age'. *auxilium adventumque dei*: 'help in the form of the appearance of a *god!*' – hendiadys* rather than hysteron proteron*.

201-4 the essence of the sentence is *maximus ultor Alcides aderat*. **tergemini**: 'threefold'. Traditionally he had three bodies; illustrations on pottery struggle to make this convincing; they show him from the side like three warriors moving in perfect time with each other. *superbus* agrees with *ultor*. **nece** ('because of') explains *superbus*: 'glorious from the killing of Geryon and his spoils'. What the *spolia* are appears in 204. **Alcides**: 'the descendant of Alcaeus'; another patronymic (103). Alcaeus was Hercules' paternal grandfather. **hac**: adv. 'this way'. *victor*: in 'apposition*' to *Alcides*, 'as victor', or translate 'in triumph'.

The huge size of the cattle comes out in the hyperbaton* including enjambment* *tauros ... ingentes*, and their number in the last phrase: they filled the valley and the riverside, i.e. the Forum Boarium and perhaps the whole valley between the Aventine and the Palatine.

205 **mens effera**: again, it is abstract noun serving as subject (cf.194): 'the maddened mind of Cacus' = 'Cacus in his madness'. **ne ... fuisset**: 'in case anything should turn out to have been ...'. A purpose clause with pluperf. subj.; ordinarily one would expect imperf. subj. It seems to suggest the thoroughness of Cacus' villainy. **inausum, intractatum**:

not only does he dare to do things, he actually does them. **sceleris** and **doli** depend on *quid*: 'anything of wickedness of trickery'; partitive gen. (NLG 201.2).

207-8 **stabulis**: 'static pasture' rather than stables. **praestanti corpore, forma superante**, abl. of description (NLG 224.1); two phrases of identical meaning, varied by choice of vocabulary and chiastic order.

209-12 Of this sentence *raptor* (211) is subj. and *occultabat* verb. **pedibus rectis** is abl. of description (NLG 224) with *qua* (n.pl.nom): '(in case there should be) any with forward-facing feet'. **forent** = *essent*. **cauda** (210): instrumental abl. 'by the tail' with *tractos*. **versis viarum indiciis**: abl. abs. 'switching the signs of the routes (they had taken)'. **saxo**: abl. of place rather than instrumental. **occultabat** imperf.: 'tried to hide'. **quaerenti**: 'to (anyone) searching (for them) ...' (dat. of reference, NLG 188.2c). (In theory it could be 'to Hercules looking for them', but nothing is made of any search by him, and when he leaves he gives no sign of knowing that he is short.) (213-4), **ferebant**: intrans. 'led'. This use of *fero* is common with *via* as subj. (*via fert ad urbem*: the road leads to town), less so without.

213 **interea**: not 'meanwhile', but 'and now' – a transition formula to a new scene'. **iam**: with *saturata*.

214-6 The *a*-alliteration* in 214 seems a decorative flourish. **abitum**: There seems no distinction at all between *abitus* and *discessus*. This, along with the observations on 207-8 and 212, suggests that Virgil is recreating in Evander the Homeric aged hero Nestor: fussy and repetitive as a speaker, but fundamentally a good person. (See also on 560.)

215 **discessu**: the abl. gives 'at the time of ...' cf. 583. **mugire** (like *impleri* and *relinqui* 216) is a historic infinitive (NLG 335), whose nearest indic. equivalent is the imperf. – here 'began to low', while *impleri* is 'were being filled' and *relinqui* 'were being abandoned'.

Virgil makes Hercules' departure a very noisy affair: three separate clauses ('tricolon'*) with three different sound-words, the second involving an enjambment* with an emphatic separation of *omne nemus*. On the one hand this is another instance of theme-and-variation; on the other it is a crescendo. The sounds get louder: the dark *ū* of *mugire* being succeeded by the brighter *ē* of *querelis* and then by the full-throated *ā* of *clamore* (abl. of attendant circumstances NLG 221), which has in addition the *cl* consonant-pair which we associate with such words as *clarus* and *clangor*. The space filled by the sound also grows, from the herd itself to the wood to the tops of the hills.

217 There is now a charming contrast between the clamour of the departing herd and the single voice raised in response. Perhaps the resonance of the *vastum antrum* was what made it audible – the enjambment* and the frequent *u-* (*v-*) sounds may encourage this idea. **boum:** gen. pl. (partitive). **sub antro:** 'down in the cave'.

218   custodita: 'imprisoned as she was'.

219-21   hic: 'at this point' (in time). The basic sentence is *Alcidae exarserat dolor*. Lit: 'Resentment had blazed up in Hercules' (*Alcidae* is dat. of reference NLG 188, as in *caput mihi dolet* – 'my head aches'). How to fit in the two abl. expressions **furiis, atro felle?** (i) take both with *exarserat*: 'because of his fury his resentment blazed with black bile'. (ii) take *atro felle* as abl. of description with *dolor*: 'his black-biled resentment blazed with madness' (Gransden). Both seem strained, (i) because *felle exarserat* is an odd mixed metaphor* (*fel* not being an inflammable substance); (ii) because *atro felle dolor* does not sound so natural a phrase as, e.g. *praestanti corpore tauros* (207). (ii) will work if we take Servius' note that *fel* is 'that by which we grow angry, according to the *physici*.' But it is perhaps a mistake to try to pin these phrases down. The essence of the passage is Hercules' uncontrolled emotion, and part of the uncontrolledness extends to the language. **exarserat**: a striking pluperf. '(It) shoots the narrative forward, as this part of it is gone by before we reach it' (Williams).

220-1 Either **arma** and **robur** are a hendiadys* for 'the oaken club which was his weapon', or *arma* refers to Hercules' other traditional weapon, his bow and arrows. In the event he uses neither. **manu**: redundant, but vivid. **nodis**: 'knots' in the wood, as four times in Virgil, but knots do not make wood heavy, so perhaps '(metal) studs' as in later epic.

221 **ardua montis**: 'the high (parts of) the hill' (partitive gen: NLG 201); 'the summit'. **aërii**: rather a baroque reference to the Aventine, judging from the way it looked in Virgil's day (i.e. approx. 150 ft high, as today). Does the legend suggest that it was originally much higher, reaching its present elevation only when Hercules smashed in the cave?

223-4 **oculis**: this could go (i) with *turbatum* – 'troubled in his eyes', 'eyes staring with terror' (Servius comments 'the eyes reveal the mind') or (ii) with *videre* (syncopated perf.) – 'our folk saw him with their own eyes'. Objections to (i): Cacus' eyes do not matter here, it is his state of mind; and Virgil's normal expression would be acc. of respect *turbatum oculos*; to (ii): *oculis* is redundant. But (i) *oculis* (local abl.) has parallels in prose, and Cacus' eyes are a matter of interest in 266, so perhaps here by anticipation; (ii) *oculis* could be like *manu* (220) redundant, but vivid.

225-7 **ut** with indic. *inclusit*: 'when'. **sese** = *se*. Vulcan had evidently provided Cacus with a rudimentary portcullis, a defensive structure known to Greeks and Romans as *catarracta* (Liv.27.28.10). The gate could be raised and lowered on its chains, but Cacus is in too much of a hurry, so he simply breaks the chains. **ferro ... et arte paterna**: hendiadys*: 'by his father's skill in iron-working'. **fultos**: lit: 'he strengthened the doorposts which were propped up on the obstacle', but translate 'he strengthened the doorposts *by propping them* up with the obstacle', i.e. the rock.

228   ecce is not strictly an imperative form, but it acts as one. Evander, the story teller, points to a feature in his story: the sudden presence of Hercules. Cacus has managed to get the doors closed by the skin of his teeth. **furens animis**: 'maddened with anger'. (*animi* pl. regularly in this sense (OLD 11); see 256.) **Tirynthius**: 'the hero from Tiryns', i.e. Hercules. Hercules' labours were performed at the instruction of Eurystheus, king of Tiryns, to whom he had had to submit as a slave after killing his own children. **omnemque**: a 'hypermetric' line (Note, p. 25), where there is an extra last syllable, which is elided against a vowel at the beginning of the following line.

229   lustrans: 'surveying'.

230   dentibus: gnashing (*infrendens*) 'with the teeth' as is the normal expression. The sequence of present participles (*furens, lustrans, infrendens*) portrays Hercules' frustration.

230-2   lustrat: something stronger than 'survey' – perhaps 'he scours' – seems appropriate here. (On *lustro* with its range of meanings see 153n.) One should be aware of the repetition, though 'Roman poets were on the whole less sensitive to such repetitions at short intervals than English poets' (P.T. Eden, commenting on 242 and 243 *penitus*).

231   Aventini: 'The city of Rome' is normally '*urbs Roma*', both words in the same case – 'apposition*'. One might expect the same here '*montem Aventinum*', but the genitive ('appositional' NLG 202) is not uncommon.

231–2 **valle**: abl. of place 'where' without preposition, cf. *luco* 271. NB change of tense: *lustrat . . . temptat . . . resedit.*

233 **stabat**: the verb begins the sentence like a new start, as Hercules looks up from where he sits in frustrated exhaustion. **silex praecisis saxis**: 'a crag with sheer cliffs all around'; *saxis* is abl. of quality (description) (NLG 224).

234 **dorso**: dat., following *insurgens* 'looming over', see NLG 187.3. **altissima visu**: 'sky-high to look at', in form like the common *mirabile dictu* (252), 'amazing to relate'; the *-u* ending is abl. of the supine, according to NLG 340 (2).

235 **nidis**: dat., translate with *opportuna*.

dirarum volucrum: *dirus* (i) 'ill-omened'. Birds which are regularly 'ill-omened' are owls: the *bubo*, the eagle-owl (*Aen*.IV.462; Ov. *Met.* XV.791) and the *strix* (Hor.*Ep.* 5.20, Tib.I.5.52); Hor. *Od.* III.27.1 might suggest we could add the *parra*, the nightjar; (ii) generally 'appalling' (*Aen*.III.228, *Aen*.VI.498), so perhaps carrion birds, vultures, crows and such. Vultures were not *dirus* in sense (i), indeed Romulus' twelve vultures constituted the good omen which led to Rome being established on the Palatine (Liv.VII.1). But they did have unpleasant associations. Seneca *Ep.*95.43: if you visit a dying person in the expectation of a legacy, you are a vulture waiting for a corpse. Cacus provided plenty of corpses (195–7). Both owls and vultures make big messy nests that could be conspicuous on the *alta silex*. All this however forms a somewhat literal-minded note, which does not do justice to the impression of horror that Virgil evidently wishes to create.

236 **hanc**: i.e. the *silex*. **ut**: 'as' with a sense of 'because': Hercules was pushing the rock the way it wanted to go. **prona iugo**: 'leaning out *from* the ridge towards (*ad*) the river'. **laevum**: Hercules was going up the Aventine from the south; we are looking at it from the north; the river is on his left. Virgil is giving us a front view of Hercules in action.

237   dexter: 'standing on its right-hand side'. **in adversum nitens**: 'straining at the side which was facing him'. **avulsam**: 'torn up', agreeing with *hanc* (236).

238   inde: 'then', 'next'.

239   impulit: 'gave it a mighty shove'. **quo** is a connecting relative (NLG 251.6 though not so called there); the normal order would be *quo impulsu*: 'with this push ...'. Virgil is wanting to put the two related words as close together as possible (polyptoton*). **maximus ... aether**: a somewhat obscure phrase, perhaps abbreviated for 'the whole space of heaven, huge as it was'.

240   refluit: the river here certainly flows backward, in contrast to the interpretation of *refluo* offered at 87.

241-2 The subjects are *specus* and *regia* (hendiadys* for the palace-cave). **detecta** agrees with *regia* but refers to both; the verb is singular, suiting the subject, which is logically if not grammatically so. **patuere**: syncopated perf.

243-6   non secus ac: 'not otherwise than ...'; 'just as', a regular phrase for introducing a simile*. *non secus ac ... dehiscens*: 'just as if the earth, split apart (*dehiscens*) deep within (*penitus*) by some force ...'. **reserat, recludat, cernatur, trepident**: all pres. subj., of possibilities unlikely to be fulfilled (NLG 303). *penitus* is repeated probably because it is a linking idea from the cave to the simile* of the underworld – a sort of anaphora*. **dis invisa**: 'hateful to the gods'. *super* here = *desuper* (*from* above); by picking the idea up in 249 Virgil invites us to concentrate on this idea as we envisage the scene. **barathrum**: a Greek word; at Athens a 'death-pit' where criminals could be thrown to die; Lucretius (III.966) used it of the pit of hell in the generation before Virgil.

245 The disgusting (*dis invisa*) pallor of the underworld may reflect the disgusting pallor of the faces of Cacus' victims (197) and encourage us to see Cacus' house as a realm of the dead and Hercules' achievement as a victory of life over death – which would justify the apocalyptic description of the struggle.

246 The spirits of the dead (*manes*) are often described as 'strengthless' (*Od*.X.521 etc.), hence their terror. In *Aen*.VI.489–93 they cowered at the sight of the living Aeneas.

248-50 The subject is *Alcides*, verb *premit* ('assails'), understood object *Cacum*; the three participles *deprensum* 'caught', *inclusum* 'trapped', *rudentem* agree with *Cacum* understood. **cavo saxo**: abl. of place where. *insueta rudentem*: 'bellowing unaccustomed (sounds)'. The accusative is 'adverbial' (NLG 176.2 Note). 'Bellowing as never before' (Williams). **telis**: *telum* can be used of a missile of any sort. **omnia arma**: 'all sorts of weapons' – not his accustomed ones. A sign of his uncontrollable fury. **molaribus**: rocks the size of millstones. This size of rock is used as weapon in Homer: *Il*.VII.270, 12.160f.

251-5 **neque enim**: 'nor indeed'. **super** = *supererat* 'was there left'. **pericli**: objective gen. (NLG.200) after *fuga* – 'any means of escaping danger'.

252 **faucibus**: abl. of separation (with *evomit* 253).

254 **oculis**: dat. 'of separation' (NLG 188 2 (d)) – translate 'from (Hercules') eyes; **glomerat**: the verb is used of getting something together in a compact mass; **sub antro**: 'down in the cave'. **fumiferam**: cf. on *paciferae* 116. **commixtis . . . tenebris**: take as abl. abs.

256 'Hercules in his anger (*animis*: see on 228) would not accept this.' **non** (or **haud**) **tulit** is a regular expression in Virgil for individuals subjected to intolerable provocation. Hercules' leap is dramatically expressed in the enjambment* of 256–7 and the very strong caesura in 257. (A similar rhythmic pattern occurs between 265 and 266.)

257–9   qua ... undam fumus agit: 'Where the most smoke drove the wave' is Virgilian for, presumably, 'the source of the wave of smoke'. NB **nebulā atrā** abl. not nom. **hic**: 'here', 'at this point'.

260   in nodum: read with *complexus*. To make the phrase break after *corripit* is to give the word some of the force that *impulit* has in 239. Then *in nodum complexus*: 'getting his hands around him knotwise' (Fordyce's word, comparing 673 *in orbem* 'in a ring' and 453 *in numerum* 'rhythmically'. The knot is a strangling one.) Then literally, 'throttled his starting eyes and blood-dry throat.' In this *elisos* and *siccum sanguine* are proleptic*: 'throttled him so that the eyes started from his head and his throat was drained of blood.' *Siccus* followed by the abl. like *vacuus* 'empty' (NLG214.1(d)).

262   foribus revulsis: Virgil does not trouble us with the question of how the *fores* relate to the portcullis (225–7).

263   'The cattle which had been stolen and the theft which had been denied on oath were shown to the heaven.' A striking line of only four words with the two heavy participle adjectives in alliteration* and 'homoioteleuton' (rhymed endings); the sense of the adj. (first in the line) *abstractae* is repeated in the noun *rapinae* (last in the line); it is the two adjectives that convey Cacus' two offences: to steal and to deny the theft.

265   'They cannot be satisfied in the hearts by gazing at. . . .' *nequeunt*: the subject is <u>not</u> *corda* (as it might seem to be on first sight), but generally 'the people' – perhaps *nostri* of line 222. *corda* is 'retained' acc. (NLG 178.2), where a word that would be the object if the verb were active (*corda vestra expleo* 'I satisfy your hearts') is kept in the acc. when the verb becomes passive (*corda explemini,* 'you are satisfied in heart'). **tuendo** instrumental 'by gazing at'. **saetis** abl.; translate closely with *villosa.* **semiferi:** cf. 194 *semihominis.*

268–74 Foundation of the altar. Some sources attribute the foundation to Hercules himself (Propertius IV.9, Ovid *Fasti* I.543–586) some to Evander (Livy I.7, Dionysius I.39–40). Either by Evander or by Hercules the Potitii and Pinarii were invited to take care of the cult. In legend the difference between their functions was explained thus. Originally both were invited on equal terms. But when the Pinarii arrived late for the feast, after the entrails had been eaten, they were punished by being for ever excluded from this part of the celebration and had to be content with the junior status to which Virgil refers by *custos.* But neither family was credited with actually founding the altar.

268 **illo:** sc. *tempore.* **celebratus (est) honos:** 'the mark of our esteem has been kept up' – *celebrare* having its root meaning of 'perform frequently'. **minores:** usually in the sense of 'later generations'. But here we know that Evander was himself present at Hercules' visit. (Later in the book he reminds Aeneas that he has entertained Hercules at his own home.) Evander is perhaps regarding those around him as being of a different generation. Of Evander's model Nestor, Homer says 'In his lifetime two generations of mortal men had already died ... and he was now ruling over the third' (*Il.*I.247–252). Or this is Evander now speaking to all time to come, so that his exhortation *quare agite, o iuvenes* (273) is addressed also to Virgil's audience.

269–271 With the punctuation as it is in the text, we must translate 'and Potitius as the first establisher and the house of Pinarius as (the first) protector set up this altar in its grove .... (*luco* abl. of place without preposition.) There are two difficulties: (i) *statuit* singular.

Either the subject is Potitius, as *auctor* (with *domus Pinaria* in brackets, as it were), or the two together are thought of as a single founding entity, as *senatus populusque Romanus* takes a singular verb. Both seem a little strained. (ii) the words *auctor* (of Potitius) and *statuit* seem to suggest a greater responsibility in establishing the cult than is anywhere else suggested.

272   quare: 'for this reason'. Evander now draws the conclusion to the thought that introduced the story of Cacus in 185–9.

273   iuvenes: he addresses Trojans and Arcadians together – see 275. **in munere** 'in appreciation of'. **laudes** are 'actions deserving praise'.

274   pōcula porgite: 'hold out' in order to pour libations, an appropriate gesture at the beginning of a celebration.

275   communemque vocate deum: 'Call on him who is god of us all'. **volentes**: 'gladly' cf. 133.

276–7   cum: 'cum inversum', as in 98–99 – 'and then'. **bicolor populus**: (distinguish *pōpulus* and *pŏpulus*) the poplar is *bicolor* with its leaves silvery grey underneath and green on top. In *Ecl.*7.61 the poplar is described as *Alcidae gratissima*. Evander's head-covering seems to be in appearance like that of sacrificing priests: a woollen circle round the head with pendants (*vittae*) either side, except that here it is made entirely of poplar sprays. 'And then the two-coloured poplar both covered his hair with Herculean shadow and, woven with leaves, hung down.' 'Herculean shadow' because of the poplar tree's association with Hercules. This may be Virgil's invention: it seems that in his day priests at the Ara Maxima wore wreaths of laurel. For -*que* . . . -*que*: see on 94.

278   scyphus: a large drinking vessel specially associated with Hercules, according to Macrobius V.21.16–17, because he was a heavy drinker and because it was in the wine-cup of the Sun that he crossed the sea to Geryon's country.

For a summary of lines 280–557, see the section on Book VIII, pp.28–30.

558–84

Evander says farewell to his son.

558 euntis: i.e. Pallas, as *pater* makes clear.

559 haeret: 'holds it fast'; see on 124. *inexpletus lacrimans*: 'weeping unstoppably'. The adverbial idea is more commonly given by the neut., and Servius offered *inexpletum* as the 'soundest' of three possibilities. But cf. V.764: *creber aspirans Auster*: 'the south wind blowing steadily'.

560–571 These lines form a very long sentence: the conditional clause (see following note) is introduced by *si* in 560, and the main sentence begins at *non ... divellerer* (568) and continues till 571. Cicero (*Orator* 222) says that a sentence should in general not be longer than four hexameters' worth; exceptional length here conveys exceptional intensity.

560 o, even when coming next to a vocative (*o iuvenes* 273), carries emotional force; more so when treated otherwise (*o quicumque es* 122) as here. *o si*: to begin with we see this as introducing a main sentence (= *utinam*), and it is something of a surprise (contributing to the overall intensity) when in 568 we find that it has been introducing a subordinate clause.

561 qualis eram: understand '... (making me) such as I was ...'. *Praeneste* (today Palestrina, a hill-town twenty-two miles east of Rome/Pallanteum) is usually neuter (VII.682), here fem. because of the idea of *urbe*. **P. sub ipsa**: 'under the very walls of P.'

562   stravi: making an enjambment* with diaeresis* between first and second foot, emphasises Evander's pride. **scutorum**: shields were normally inflammable – made of leather on a wooden framework. Homeric warriors proudly profited from captured spoils (Hector wore Achilles' armour taken from Patroclus). Evander, in burning his spoils, adheres to a Roman tradition attributed to Tarquinius Priscus, fifth king of Rome (Livy I.37.5). **scutorum ... acervos**: 'heaps of shields', but the stress falls on *acervos* (at line-end, hyperbaton* with *scutorum*) so perhaps trs. '... shields in heaps'. **victor**: in apposition to understood *ego*: 'as victor', or trs. 'in victory'.

563   Erulum: Erulus appears nowhere else in surviving literature; he may well be invented by Virgil for the occasion. **sub + acc.**: 'down to'. **Tartara**: perhaps stronger than 'Hades'.

564–7 '... to whom at his birth his mother Feronia had given three lives, ... three sets of armour to wield – three times he had to be laid low in death, and yet from him at that time this hand took all his lives and stripped him as many times of his weapons.' **cui** in 564 is indirect object of *dederat*, *cui* in 566 is 'dative of separation' (NLG188 2(d)). 564–6 are held together by the anaphora* *tres ... terna ... ter*. There is a change of construction (anacoluthon* – NLG 374.6) by which for the third element (*ter ...*) the subj. changes from *mater* to Erulus himself.

tres animas: Servius notes that in being given three lives Erulus was being made into another Geryon, hence Evander into another Hercules. **Fērōnia**: a goddess widely known in central Italy with a grove at Rome dating to the late third century BCE.

The differences which follow from 'three lives' (564) as opposed to 'three bodies' (Geryon) are left to our imagination, which is encouraged to work by the exclamation *horrendum* ('shudder-worthy') *dictu*, for which cf. *mirabile dictu* (252). **leto**: *letum* is used in the *Aeneid* less than half as often as *mors*; sometimes it seems to be used for the sake of euphony, sometimes because it seems a more solemn word; it always refers to violent death.

568 divellerer: imperf. subj. of *present* unrealised possibility, vividly responding to the wish for *future* fulfilment in *referat* (560). **usquam**: 'anywhere' – i.e. 'least of all as you went to war'; **umquam** at the end of 561 means we have 'at no place, at no time' – 'passionate emphasis' (Page).

569–71 huic capiti insultans: *insulto* is literally 'to trample on' (A.12.339 – of Turnus – *caesis hostibus insultans*: 'trampling on his slaughtered enemies'), thus, even as a metaphor*, much stronger than Eng. 'insult'. *Caput* 'person' as in 145. *Hic* is used to refer to oneself. **finitimo**: '(me, his) neighbour'; dative obj. of *insultans*. **dedisset . . . funera**: 'caused so many dreadful deaths with the sword' (OLD24). The alliteration* *ferro – funera* holds the phrase together over the enjambment*. *tot . . . tam* form a sort of anaphora* of exclamatory adverbs. *viduasset*: short form ('syncope' see p. 25) of pluperf. subj. *viduavisset*. **civibus** is abl. of separation (NLG 214(b)).

finitimo: The word can hardly be being used to aggravate Mezentius' offence. (On Mezentius, see the summary of lines 454ff, p. 29.) It is normal for wars to be fought between neighbours, and the idea of charity towards one's neighbour comes to us not from any classical source, but from English translations of such passages as Matthew 19.19. Rather, it is the expression of Evander's distress at his inability to perform the most basic duty of a king: to keep the neighbours at bay. But Evander's description of Mezentius (481–491) suggests that his violence was enacted entirely on his own people, not his neighbours, even though fellow-feeling among the Etruscans prompts them all to demand that the Rutuli surrender Mezentius (494–5). So it is a new idea when he seems to suggest (570–1) that Pallanteum has suffered at Mezentius' hands. (571 *urbem* is surely Pallanteum not Caere:

Evander can hardly be taking responsibility for Mezentius' brutality there.) But Virgil is not consistent on the state of peace or war in Italy: VII.46 'Evander had been ruling during a long period of peace'; VIII.55: Evander's Arcadians 'are at constant war with the Latins'.

572   divum gen. pl. *deus.*

573   Arcadii: it is not immediately obvious why Evander makes a point about his origin in appealing to Jupiter – unless perhaps we are intended to think of traditions about Arcadia such as are mentioned by the Greek travel-writer Pausanias (second century CE): 'Because of their justice and religion the [Arcadians of ancient time] entertained gods and sat at table with them, and the gods visibly rewarded their goodness with favour and their wickedness with wrath' (VIII.2.4 trs. Levi).

574–5   Think si numina vestra, si fata mihi incolumem Pallanta reservant: 'If your spirits and if the fates are keeping Pallas safe for me'. *reservare:* 'to keep some(one) safe for a greater purpose'.

576   si visurus eum vivo: 'if I am living with the prospect of seeing him . . .'. **in unum:** 'to the same (place)', 'together'.

577   patior, often meaning 'I allow' here takes on 'I agree'; **laborem** is obj. of *durare,* which elsewhere in Virgil is intransitive. *perferre* would have fitted the verse here; Virgil evidently wanted the extra idea of *durus* – 'hard'.

578   aliquem . . . casum: Evander cannot bring himself to express the alternative to Pallas' safe return, as he acknowledges with *infandum.* **Fortuna:** the gods and destiny would be responsible for Pallas' safe return (574–5), but Evander cannot bear to suggest that they might be responsible for his death: it would have to be Fortuna, who distributes good and bad merely on a whim (Horace, *Odes* I.35.1–4). This clear distinction between *fatum* and *fortuna* is rather different from VIII.334, where the two have combined to bring Evander to Pallanteum.

579   o: see note on 560; here it simply intensifies *liceat* 'may I be allowed' – jussive subjunctive (NLG 275 1).

580-2   dum curae ambiguae (sunt): 'while my anxieties point in different directions'. **dum . . . futuri** (*est*): *spes* here 'expectation' rather than 'hope' (OLD2); *futuri* depends on it: 'expectation of what is to come'. **mea sola et sera voluptas**: 'my only delight at the end of my life'. *complexu*: 'in' or 'with' –instrumental or 'place where'. **gravior . . . vulneret**: 'and let no news too grim injure my ears', carrying the sense on from 579, with the idea 'were I dead, no news would come . . .'. The comparative of an adjective *x* often suggests 'on the *x* side'. 'too *x*': *senectus est natura loquacior*: 'old age is too talkative' (Cicero, *Cato Minor* 55).

583-4   genitor: Evander's long speech only became directed specifically to Pallas in 581; this word reminds us. **digressu**: abl. as *discessu* 215; the word is different from *discessus* in having more of a sense of parting'(from verb *di-gredior* 'move apart').**fundebat. . .ferebant**: 'The imperfects are to be noticed, showing that the old man fails and is carried away while he is yet speaking' (Conington).

Vocabulary

Long vowels are marked with a macron '–', all others are short. The 'short' symbol '˘' is used to draw attention to a quantity that might be misread. Adjectives are shown **either** with other genders of nom. sing, as many as they have, **or**, if they have only one nom. sing. form, with the gen. sing. An asterisk indicates that the word appears in the OCR Defined Vocabulary List for AS.

*ā *or* ab *prep. + abl.*	by, from
abiēs abiĕtis *f.*	fir
abitus -ūs *m.*	departure
abiūrō abiūrāre abiūrāvī abiūrātum	deny on oath
abrumpō abrumpere abrūpī abruptum	break off, cut short
abstrahō abstrahere abstraxī abstractum	remove
*abstulī *see* auferō	
*absum abesse āfuī	be absent, be missing
*ac *conj.*	and; 243: 'than'
*accēdō accēdere accessī accessum	approach
accessus -ūs *m.*	way in
*accipiō accipere accēpī acceptum	receive, welcome
acernus -a -um *adj.*	made of maple wood
acervus -ī *m.*	heap
*aciēs aciēī *f.*	battle-line
acūtus -a -um *adj.*	sharp
*ad *prep. + acc.*	(i) to, towards (ii) at, near

*addō addere addidī additum	add
*adferō adferre attulī adlātum	bring, contribute
adfīgō adfīgere adfīxī adfīxum	fix
adfor adfārī adfātus sum	speak to, address
*adlābor adlābī adlāpsus sum	move smoothly (towards)
*adloquor adloquī adlocūtus	address, speak to
sum	
adluō adluere adluī	wash
adsuēscō adsuēscere adsuēvī	tr accustom *or* intr become
adsuētum	accustomed
*adsum adesse adfuī	be present
*advehor advehī advectus sum	travel to
adventus -ūs *m.*	arrival
*adversus -a -um *adj.*	opposite, facing
*advertō advertere advertī	turn (sg.) towards
adversum *tr.*	
*advocō advocāre advocāvī	summon up
advocātum	
Aenēās Aenēae *acc.* Aenēān	Aeneas
aequō aequāre aequāvī	make equal
aequātum	
aequor aequoris *n.*	smooth surface, water
āērius -a -um *adj.*	lofty
aestuō aestuāre aestuāvī	seethe
aestuātum	
aetās aetātis *f.*	time, age
aethēr aethĕris *m.*	upper air, sky
aetherius -a -um *adj.*	celestial
āfore *fut. infin.* absum	
agnōscō agnōscere agnōvī	recognize
agnitum	
*agō agere ēgī āctum	do, drive; **agite:** come on now!

āiō ăit	say
āla -ae *f.*	wing
Alcīdēs Alcīdae *acc.* **Alcīdēn**	*another name for* Hercules (see on 203)
aliquandō *adv.*	at long last
aliquī -qua -quod *adj.*	some (person/thing)
***altus -a -um** *adj.*	high, tall
ambiguus -a -um *adj.*	doubtful
ambō ambae ambō *pron.*	both
***amīcus -a -um** *adj.*	friendly
amnis amnis *m.*	river
***amor amōris** *m.*	love, longing
Amphitryōniadēs Amphitryōniadae	son of Amphitryon, i.e. Hercules
amplector amplectī amplexus sum	embrace
amplexus -ūs *m.*	embrace
***an** *conj. in questions*	or?
Anchīsēs Anchīsae	Anchises, Aeneas' father
angō angere anxī anctum	throttle
anima -ae *f.*	life, breath
***animus -ī** *m.*	mind, spirit; *pl.* **animī** high spirits, anger, courage
***annus -ī** *m.*	year
annuus -a -um *adj.*	annual
***ante** *prep.* + *acc.*	before, in front of
antrum -ī *n.*	cave
appāreō appārēre appāruī appāritum	appear
***aqua -ae** *f.*	water
***āra -ae** *f.*	altar
***arbor arboris** *f.*	tree

Arcadia -ae	Arcadia, a region in Greece, Evander's home
Arcadius -a -um	Arcadian
ardeō ardēre arsī arsum	burn, blaze
arduus -a -um *adj.*	steep, high up
***arma armōrum** *n.pl.*	arms
armentum -ī *n.*	herd
***ars artis** *f.*	craft, skill
arx arcis *f.*	stronghold, citadel
aspiciō aspicere aspexī aspectum	look at
***at** *conj.*	but
āter ātra ātrum *adj.*	black, dark
Atlāntis *abl.* **Atlāntide**	daughter of Atlas
Atlās Atlāntis	Atlas, the giant who holds up the sky
***atque** *conj.*	and, *or* and indeed
Atrīdae Atrīdārum	the sons of Atreus, Agamemnon and Menelaus
***attulit** *see* **adferō**	
auctor auctōris *m.*	originator
***audāx audācis** *adj.*	daring
***audiō audīre audīvī audītum**	hear
***auferō auferre abstulī ablātum**	take away
aureus -a -um *adj.*	golden
auris auris *f.*	ear
aurum -ī *n.*	gold
***aut** *conj.*	or
***autem** *particle*	but, what is more
***auxilium -ī** *n.*	help, reinforcement
āvellō āvellere āvellī/āvulsī āvulsum	tear up

Aventīnus -ī	the Aventine (hill)
āvertō āvertere āvertī āversum	steal
Bacchus -ī	Bacchus, the wine god, the Greek Dionysus; 181 'wine'
barathrum -ī *n.*	abyss (245)
***bellum -ī** *n.*	war
bicolor bicolōris *adj.*	two-coloured
bīnī -ae -a *adj.*	two
bōs bovis *m. or f.*	cow, bull, ox
Cācus -ī	Cacus, son of Vulcan; the giant killed by Hercules
cadāver cadāveris *n.*	corpse
caecus -a -um *adj.*	blind
***caedēs caedis** *f.*	blood
***caelum -ī** *n.*	sky
cālīgō cālīginis *f.*	darkness
candidus -a -um *adj.*	pure white, bright, fair
canistra -ae *f.*	basket
***caput capitis** *n.*	head, person
carīna -ae *f.*	keel, ship
***cārus -a -um** *adj.*	dear
cāsus -ūs *m.*	chance, accident
catēna -ae *f.*	chain
cauda -ae *f.*	tail
***causa -ae** *f.*	cause
caverna -ae *f.*	hollow space, cavern
cavus -a -um *adj.*	hollow
celebrō celebrāre celebrāvī celebrātum	celebrate, observe

celerō celerāre celerāvī celerātum *tr. & intr.*	hasten
celsus -a -um *adj.*	lofty
Cerēs Cereris	Ceres, the corn goddess, to the Greeks Demeter; 181 'bread'
*cernō cernere crēvī crētum	see, notice
certātim *adv.*	in competition
chlamys chlamydis *f.*	light cloak
*cingō cingere cīnxī cīnctum	surround, encircle
*cīvis -is *m. or f.*	citizen
*clāmŏr clāmōris *m.*	shouting, noise
cognātus -a -um *adj.*	related by blood
collis -is *m.*	hill
coma -ae *f.*	hair
commisceō commiscēre commiscuī commixtum	mix up
commūnis commūne *adj.*	common, shared
compellō compellāre compellāvī compellātum	speak to, address
complector complectī complexus sum	enfold, embrace, clasp
complexus -ūs *m.*	embrace
comprimō comprimere compressī compressum	suppress
cōmptus -a -um *ppl* cōmō	adorned, dressed
concipiō concipere concēpī conceptum	conceive
concutiō -ere -cussī -cussum	shake
*coniungō coniungere coniūnxī coniūnctum	join
conlābor conlābī conlāpsus sum	collapse

cōnscendō cōnscendere cōnscendī cōnscēnsum	climb up to
*cōnspiciō cōnspicere cōnspexī cōnspectum	catch sight of
*cōnsurgō cōnsurgere cōnsurrēxī cōnsurrēctum	rise, get up
cor cordis *n.*	heart
cōram *adv.*	face to face
*corpus corporis *n.*	body
*corripiō corripere corripuī correptum	seize
crāstinus -a -um *adj.*	tomorrow's
*crēdō crēdere crēdidī crēditum + *dat.*	believe
crētus -a -um *adj., ppl.* crēscō (135)	born (from)
*crūdēlis crūdēle *adj.*	brutal, savage
cruŏr cruŏris *m.*	blood (*from a wound*)
*cum	(i) *prep.* + *abl.* with, accompanying (ii) *conj.* when, since; **cum prīmum** as soon as
*cūnctī -ae -a *adj.*	all
*cupidus -a -um *adj.*	eager
*cūra -ae *f.*	care, anxiety
cursus -ūs *m.*	run, running
*custōdiō custōdīre custōdīvī/iī custōdītum	guard
*custōs custōdis *m. or f.*	guard, guardian
Cyllēnē Cyllēnae	Cyllene, a mountain in Arcadia
Danăī Danaōrum	Danai, another name for the Greeks

daps dapis *f.*   feast

Dardania -ae   Dardania, the land of Troy

Dardanus -ī   Dardanus, son of Jupiter, ancestor
                                         of the Trojans

Daunius -a -um   'associated with Daunus'. Daunus
                                         was Turnus' father.

dehīscō dehīscere   split apart

***dēiciō dēicere dēiēcī**   cast down
dēiectum

dēns dentis *m.*   tooth

dēprendō dēprendere   catch
dēprendī dēprēnsum

dēserō dēserere dēseruī   abandon
dēsertum

dēsuper *adv.*   from above

***dētegō dētegere dētēxī**   uncover
dētēctum

***deus -ī** *m. gen. pl.* **deōrum,** god
deum *dat., abl. pl.* **dīs**

***dexter -tra -trum** *adj.*   right (*side*); on the right (237)

***dextra -ae** *f.* (*sc.* **manus**) right hand

***dīcō dīcere dixī dictum**   say

dictum -ī *n.*   word

dīditus -a -um *adj., ppl.* **dīdō** spread abroad, diffused

***diēs diēī** *m. and f.*   day

differō differre distulī dīlātum   postpone

dīgressus -ūs *m.*   parting

***dīmittō dīmittere dīmīsī**   send away
dīmissum

***dīrus -a -um** *adj*   dreadful

***discēdō discēdere discessī**   depart
discessum

discessus -ūs *m.*	departure
disiciō disicere disiēcī disiectum	scatter, throw apart
dissultō -āre dissultāvī	leap apart
dīvellō dīvellere dīvellī/ dīvulsī dīvulsum	tear apart
dīvus -ī *gen.pl* dīvum	god
*dō dare dedī datum	give, offer, cause (570)
*dolŏr -ōris *m.*	pain, grief, resentment
*dolus -ī *m.*	trick
*domus -ūs *and* -ī *f.*	house, home
*dōnum -ī *n.*	gift
dorsum -ī *n.*	ridge
ductŏr ductōris *m.*	leader
*dūcō -ere duxī ductum	lead, guide
dulcis dulce *adj.*	sweet
*dum *conj.*	while
dūrō dūrāre dūrāvī dūrātum	endure
*dux ducis *m.*	leader
*ē *or* ex *prep.* + *abl.*	from, out of, arising from
*eā *see* is ea id	
ecce *interj.*	look!
ēdō ēdere ēdidī ēditum	produce; 136: give birth to
edō esse ēdī ēsum	eat
efferus -a -um *adj.*	savage
*ēgī *see* agō	
*ego mē (mei) mihi mē *pron.*	I, me
*ēgredior ēgredī ēgressus sum	come out, disembark
Ēlectra -ae	Electra, daughter of Atlas, mother of Dardanus

ēlīdō ēlīdere ēlīsī ēlīsum	knock out
*ēmūniō ēmūnīre ēmūniī ēmūnītum	strengthen
*enim *particle*	(i) *explanatory* for (*2nd in clause*) (ii) *asseverative* yes!
*eō īre iī/īvī ītum	go
equidem = ego quidem	I for my part
*ergō *conj.*	therefore
*ēripiō ēripere ēripuī ēreptum	snatch, take away
Erulus -ī	Erulus, king of Praeneste
*et *conj.*	and, even, et . . . et both . . . and
Euandrus -ī	Evander, king of Pallanteum on the site of future Rome
*euntis	*gen. sing. pres. part.* eō
Eurus -ī	Eurus, the east wind
ēvomō ēvomere ēvomuī ēvomitum	spew out
*ex = ē	
exardēscō exardēscere exarsī exarsum	blaze up
*excipio excipere excēpī exceptum	receive, welcome
eximō eximere exēmī exemptum	remove
expleō explēre explēvī explētum	fill, satisfy
exstinguō exstinguere exstinxī exstinctum	extinguish
exta extōrum *n.pl.*	entrails, offal
extemplō *adv.*	immediately
*exterritus -a -um	terrified

extimēscō extimēscere extimuī	be greatly afraid
exuō exuere exuī exūtum	strip
faciēs faciēī *f.*	appearance, face
*****faciō facere fēcī factum**	make, do; perform sacrifice
*****fallō fallere fefellī falsum**	deceive
*****fāma -ae** *f.*	reputation, fame
famēs famis *f.*	hunger
famulus -ī *m.*	slave
fatīgō fatīgāre fatīgāvī	wear out
fatīgātum *tr.*	
fātum -ī *or* **fāta -ōrum** *n.pl.*	fate, destiny
faucēs faucium *f.pl.*	throat, jaws
*****faveō favēre fāvī fautum**	show favour or good will
fel fellis *n.*	bile
*****ferō ferre tulī lātum**	carry, bear, tolerate
Fērōnia -ae	Feronia, Italian goddess, mother
	of Erulus
*****ferrum -ī** *n.*	iron, sword
fervidus -a -um *adj.*	boiling
fessus -a -um *adj.*	weary
*****fidēs fideī** *f.*	good faith, honour, trust; 150:
	'promise'
*****fīlius -ī** *m.*	son
*****fīnēs -ium** *m.*	borders, territory
fīnitimus -a -um *adj.*	neighbouring
flexus -ūs *m.*	curve
flōs flōris *m.*	flower, bloom
fluvius -ī *m.*	river, stream, current
*****foedus foederis** *n.*	treaty
folium -ī *n.*	leaf
for fārī fātus sum	say, speak

forem forēs foret *etc.*	*used as equivalent to* **essem** *etc.,*
	impf. subj. of **sum**
forēs forum *f.pl*	door
forma -ae *f.*	shape, beauty
***forte** *adv.*	by chance
***fortis forte** *adj.*	strong, brave
Fortūna -ae	the goddess Fortune
frēnum -ī *n.*	bridle
frētus -a -um *adj.* + *abl.*	relying on
frōns frondis *f.*	foliage
***fuga -ae** *f.*	escape
***fugiō fugere fūgī fugitum**	flee
fulciō fulcīre fulsī fultum	support, prop up
fulgeō fulgēre fulsī	shine, gleam
fūmifer -a -um *adj.*	smoke-bearing, smoky
fūmō fūmāre fūmāvī	steam, smoke
fūmus -ī *m.*	smoke
***fundō fundere fūdī fūsum**	pour; give birth to (139)
fūnus fūneris *n.*	death
fūr fūris *m.*	thief
furiae -ārum *f.pl.*	madness
furō furere	rage
***futūrus -a -um** *adj., fut. part.*	
sum	
futūrum -ī *n.*	the future
gelidus -a -um *adj.*	icy
geminī geminōrum *m.pl.*	twin, 'the two ...'
gena -ae *f.*	cheek
generō generāre generāvī	beget
generātum	
genitŏr genitōris *m.*	father

*gēns gentis *f.*	nation, people, clan
*genus generis *n.*	race, nation, kind
Gēryonēs Gēryonae	Geryon, giant of the far west killed by Hercules
glomerō glomerāre glomerāvī glomerātum	accumulate, make a ball of
Grāiugena -ae *gen.pl.* Grāiugenum	Greek
grāmineus -a -um *adj.*	grassy, made of turf
*gravis grave *adj.*	heavy, serious, grim
gravō gravāre gravāvī gravātum	make heavy, load
guttur gutturis *n.*	throat
*habeō habēre habuī habitum	have, possess
hāc *adv.*	this way
haereō haerēre haesī haesum *intr.*	stick fast, hold tightly to
Herculeus -a -um	'of Hercules'
Hēsiona -ae	Hesione, sister of Priam
Hesperia -ae	Hesperia, 'the Western Land', Italy
*hic haec hoc hūius *pron.*	this
*hīc *adv.*	here
*honōs (*also* honŏr) honōris *m.*	(mark of) honour
horreō horrēre horruī	shudder
*hospes hospitis *m.*	guest
*hūc *adv.*	(to) here, hither
*humus -ī *f.*	ground
*iaciō iacere iēcī iactum	throw
*iam *adv.*	already, now
iamdūdum *adv.*	for some time now

**īdem eadem idem *pron.*	the same
ignārus -a -um *adj.*	ignorant
igneus -a -um *adj.*	fiery
*ignis ignis *m.*	fire
ignōtus -a -um *adj.*	unknown, unfamiliar
Īliacus -a -um	Trojan
īlicet *adv.*	immediately
*ille illa illud illīus *pron.*	that (person etc.)
illūc *f.*	there, thither
immānis immāne *adj.*	huge and dreadful
*immittō immittere immīsī immissum	introduce, inflict
*impellō impellere impulī impulsum	shove
impleō implēre implēvī implētum	fill
*impōnō impōnere imposuī impositum	impose
impulsus -ūs *m.*	shove
*īmus -a -um *adj.*	lowest, bottom of
*in	(i) *prep.* + *acc.* into (ii) *prep.* + *abl.* in
inaccessus -a -um *adj.*	unapproachable
inausus -a -um *adj.*	unventured
*incendium -ī *n.*	fire
*incendō incendere incendī incēnsum *tr.*	burn
*incertus -a -um *adj.*	uncertain
*incipiō incipere incēpī inceptum *tr.*	begin
inclūdō inclūdere inclūsī inclūsum	shut in, trap

incolumis incolume *adj.*	safe, unharmed
incumbō incumbere	lean on, lean towards, work
incubuī + *dat.*	hard at
***inde** *conj.*	thence, then
indicium -ī *n.*	evidence, sign
inexplētus -a -um	insatiable
īnfandus -a -um *adj.*	unspeakable
īnfernus -a -um *adj.*	lower
īnformis -e *adj.*	shapeless, ugly
***īnfrā** *adv.*	below
īnfrendō īnfrendere	gnash
***ingēns ingentis** *adj.*	huge
inhaereō inhaerēre inhaesī	cling to
inhaesum	
***inimīcus -a -um** *adj.*	hostile
innectō innectere innexuī	entwine
innexum	
innō innāre	float
inops inopis *adj.*	poor, needy
***inquam inquis inquit**	say
***īnsequor īnsequī īnsecūtus**	harass, pursue
sum	
***īnsignis īnsigne** *adj.*	remarkable, conspicuous
īnspērātus -a -um *adj.*	unexpected
īnstō īnstāre īnstitī	threaten, attack
īnsuētus -a -um *adj.*	unaccustomed, strange
īnsultō īnsultāre īnsultāvī	show contempt for (+ *dat.*)
īnsultātum	
***īnsurgō īnsurgere īnsurrēxī**	rise above
***inter** *prep.* + *acc.*	between, among
***intereā** *adv.*	meanwhile
intertextus -a -um *adj.*	inwoven

intonō intonāre intonuī	thunder
intractātus -a -um *adj.*	not undertaken
invideō invidēre -vīdī -vīsum	hate
invīsō invīsere invīsī invīsum	visit
*invītō invītāre invītāvī	entertain
invītātum	
involvō involvere involvī	wrap up, enfold
involūtum	
*ipse -a -um ipsius *emphatic*	himself (her-, it-)
pron.	
*īra -ae *f.*	anger
*is ea id eius *pron.*	this, that, the; he, she, it; they,
	them
*ita *adv.*	so
*iter itineris *n.*	journey
*iubeō -ēre iussī iussum	order
iugum -ī *n.*	yoke, ridge
*iungō iungere iunxī iunctum	join
*Iuppiter Iovis	Jupiter
iuvenālis iuvenāle *adj.*	youthful
iuvenca -ae *f.*	heifer
*iuvenis iuvenis *m.*	young man
iuventās iuventātis *f.*	youth (*time of life*)
iuventūs iuventūtis *f.*	youth, young people collectively
*iuvō iuvāre iūvī iūtum	help
*lābor lābī lāpsus sum	slip, glide
*labŏr labōris *m.*	trouble, misfortune
*labōrō labōrāre labōrāvī	toil (181: *tr.* toil at)
labōrātum *intr.*	
lacrimō lacrimāre lacrimāvī	weep
lacrimātum	

*laetus -a -um *adj.*	cheerful
laevus -a -um *adj.*	on the left
Lāomedontiadēs	son of Laomedon, i.e. Priam
Lāomedontiadae	
Latīnī -ōrum	the Latins, inhabitants of Latium
*laus laudis *f.*	praise, glory
*lēgātus -ī *m.*	envoy, representative
*legō legere lēgī lēctum	choose
lēniō lēnīre lēnīvī/lēniī	make calm
lēnītum	
leō leōnis *m.*	lion
lētum -ī *n.*	death
*libēns *participle as adv.*	gladly, willingly
lībō lībāre lībāvī lībātum	pour a libation
*licet licēre licuit *impers.*	it is permitted
līmen līminis *n.*	threshold, door
locō locāre locāvī locātum	place
*longus -a -um *adj.*	long; *adv.* **longē** over a long distance
*loquor loquī locūtus sum	speak
luctāmen luctāminis *n.*	effort
lūcus -ī *m.*	grove
lūmen lūminis *n.*	gaze
lūstrālis lūstrāle *adj.*	sacrificial
lūstrō lūstrāre lūstrāvī	go over, purify, gaze at (153)
lūstrātum	
*lūx lūcis *f.*	light
Lycius -a -um	from Lycia in south-west Turkey
*magnus -a -um *adj.*	great
Maia -ae	Maia, daughter of Atlas, mother of Mercury

Mānēs Mānium	the Manes, the spirits of the dead
***manus -ūs** f.*	hand
***mare maris** n.*	sea
***maximus -a -um** adj., superl. of*	
magnus	
***mē** pron., acc. of* **ego**	me
***medius -a -um** adj.*	middle of ...
meminī meminisse	remember
***mēns mentis** f.*	mind, heart
mēnsa -ae f.	table
Mercurius -ī	the god Mercury
meritus -a -um adj.	well-deserved
***meus -a -um** adj.*	my
Mēzentius -ī	Mezentius, lord of Caere in Etruria, most brutal of Turnus' allies
***mihi** and **mihī** pron., dat.*	(to) me
of **ego**	
ministrō ministrāre	serve, provide
ministrāvī ministrātum	
***minor minārī minātus sum**	threaten
***minor minus** adj. comp. of*	smaller, lesser, younger
parvus	
***mīrābilis mīrābile** adj.*	astonishing
***mīror mīrārī mīrātus sum**	be amazed, admire
miserēscō miserēscere + *gen.*	take pity on
mītis mīte adj.	gentle, calm
***mittō mittere mīsī missum**	send; bring (148)
***moenia moenium** n.*	walls, fortifications
molāris molāris m.	millstone, boulder
mōlēs mōlis f.	mass
***mōns montis** m.*	mountain

mōnstrum -ī *n.*	portent, monster
***mōs mōris** *m.*	manner
***moveō movēre mōvī** **mōtum** *tr.*	move
mūgiō mūgīre mūgīvī/mūgiī **mūgītum**	low, bellow
***multī -ae -a** *adj.*	many
***mūnus mūneris** *n.*	reward, appreciation
***mūrus -ī** *m.*	wall

***nam** *conj.*	for
***nāscor nāscī nātus sum**	be born
nātus -ī *m.*	son
***nē** *conj.*	(i) *in purpose clauses:* so that ... not (ii) *in wishes:* let not ...
***-ne?**	*particle indicating open question*
nebula -ae *f.*	cloud, fog
nefās *n.* *(indeclinable)*	wickedness, crime
nemus nemoris *n.*	wood, trees
***neque ... neque** *conj.*	neither ... nor
nequeō nequīre	be unable
nēquīquam *adv.*	in vain
neu = et nē *conj.*	(181) and let not ...
nex necis *f.*	killing
nīdus -ī *m.*	nest
***nihil -ī** *n.* *pron.*	nothing
nītor -ī	strain
***nōbīscum**	with us
nōdus -ī *m.*	knot
***nōmen nōminis** *n.*	name
***nōn** *adv.*	not
***nōs nōs (nostrum) nōbis** *pron.*	we, us

*noster nostra nostrum *adj.	our
novō novāre novāvī novātum	renew; do as new
*nox noctis *f.	night
*nullus -a -um *gen. *nullius, *dat.	no (as in 'no lions': **nulli leones**)
nulli *adj.*	
nūmen nūminis *n.*	divine spirit
*nunc *adv.*	now
*nuntius -ī *m.*	messenger, news
ō *interj.*	O!
ōbex ōbicis *f.*	bar, obstacle (*on the quantity of the 'o' see *227*n*)
obiciō obicere obiēcī obiectum	put (*x*) in the way
obstipēscō obstipēscere obstipuī	be astounded
obvius -a -um *adj.*	in the way, 'to meet'
occultō occultāre occultāvī occultātum	conceal
ōcior *comp. adj. with no positive;* adv. ōcius (101)	quicker; rather quickly
*oculus -ī *m.*	eye
olīva -ae *f.*	olive (-tree)
ollī = illī	
*omnis omne *adj.*	all
onerō onerāre onerāvī onerātum	load (x *with* y, or y *into* x)
opācus -a -um *adj.*	dark, shadowy
opēs opum *f.*	wealth
opportūnus -a -um *adj.*	suitable
*optimus -a -um *adj., sup. of* bonus	best, excellent

optō optāre optāvī optātum	long for, wish for
orāculum -ī	oracle
orbis orbis *m.*	circle, disc, ring, sphere
*ōrō ōrāre ōrāvī ōrātum	pray (for)
*ōs ōris *n.*	face
*ostendō ostendere ostendī ostēnsum/ostentum	show

pācifer -fera -ferum *adj.*	peace-bringing
Pallās Pallantis	Pallas, Evander's son
pallidus -a -um *adj.*	pale, discoloured
palūs palūdis *f.*	fen, area of standing water
pandō pandere — passum/pānsum	spread wide, open
pangō pangere pepigī pāctum	settle on (?) (143: see note)
*parēns parentis *m. or f.*	parent
*parō parāre parāvī parātum	prepare
*pater patris *m.*	father
paternus -a -um *adj.*	a father's, paternal
*patior patī passus sum	suffer, permit, agree (577)
patrius -a -um *adj.* = paternus	
*paucī -ae -a *adj.*	few
*pauper pauperis *adj.*	poor, impoverished
*pāx pācis *f.*	peace
pectus pectoris *n.*	breast, heart
pellis pellis *f*	hide, skin
*pellō pellere pepulī pulsum	drive off
penātēs penātium *m.*	household gods, home
pendeō pendēre pependī *intr.*	hang
penitus *adv.*	utterly, deep down
pependit *see* pendeō	
*per *prep.* + *acc.*	through, by means of

percutiō percutere percussī	strike
percussum	
perhibeō perhibēre perhibuī	testify
perhibitum	
***perīc(u)lum** *n.*	danger
perpetuus -a -um *adj.*	continuous
***pēs pedis** *m.*	foot
***petō petere petīvī/petiī**	seek, look for
petītum	
pharetra -ae *f.*	quiver
Phenĕus -ī	Pheneus, a city in Arcadia
pictus -a -um *adj. pp.* **pingō**	paint, colour
Pīnārius -a -um *adj.*	belonging to the family of
	Pinarius (270)
pius -a -um *adj.*	good (84, note)
placidus -a -um *adj.*	pleasant, calm, tranquil
***plūrimus -a -um** *adj., superl.*	most
of **multus**	
pōculum -ī *n.*	cup
pōpulus -ī *f.*	poplar-tree
porgō (274) = **porrigō**	hold out
porrigere porrēxī porrēctum	
postis postis *m.*	doorpost
***postquam** *conj.*	after, when
potentia -ae *f.*	power
Potītius -ī	Potitius (269)
praeceps praecipitis *adj.*	headlong, sheer
praecipuus -a -um *adj.*	special
praecīsus -a -um *adj.*	cut away, sheer
Praeneste Praenestis	Praeneste, a hill-town south-east
	of Rome
praestāns praestantis *adj.*	excellent

praetendō praetendere praetendī praetentum	hold out
praeteritus -a -um *adj.*	past
precēs precum *f.pl.* (*sing.* prex *not found*)	prayer
*precor precārī precātus sum	pray
premō premere pressī pressum	press, harass
Priamus -ī	Priam, king of Troy
*prīmum *adv.*	for the first time
*prīmus -a -um *adj.*	first
*procul *adv.*	far away
profugus -a -um *adj.*	fleeing *or as noun* refugee
*prōgredior prōgredī prōgressus sum	move forward
prōnus -a -um *adj.*	leaning forward
propinquō propinquāre propinquāvī + *dat.*	approach
prōra -ae *f.*	prow
prōspectus -ūs *m.*	sight
prōtinus *adv.*	straightaway; directly on (from)
*prōtrahō prōtrahere prōtraxī prōtractum	drag out
*puer -ī *m.*	boy
puppis puppis *f.*	stern (of a ship), ship
quā *adv.*	where
*quaerō -ere quaesīvī quaesītum	seek, look for
quaesō (*only in pres.*)	I beg
*quālis quāle *adj.*	like, such as
*quam *adv.*	as

*quandō *conj.	when, since
quārē *conj.*	for this reason
*quattuor	four
*-que *conj.*	and
querēla -ae	complaint, plaintive sound
*quī quae quod cūius *pron.*	who, which, *also adj.* what? which?
quīcumque quaecumque quodcumque *pron.*	whoever, whatever
quīn *conj.*	so that ... not (148)
*quis quid cūius *pron.*	(i) (*question*) who? what? (ii) (*indef.*) anyone, anything
*quisquam quicquam *pron.*	(not) anyone, anything
quīvīs quaevīs quodvīs *pron.*	any ('any you care to name')
*quō *adv.*	where to? whither?
*quod *conj.*	because, that
radius -ī *m.*	ray
rādīx rādīcis *f.*	root
rāmus -ī *m.*	branch
rapīna -ae *f.*	theft
*rapiō rapere rapuī raptum	seize, grasp
raptŏr raptōris *m.*	plunderer
rārus -a -um *adj.*	scattered
ratis ratis *f.*	ship
*recēns recentis *adj.*	fresh
recessus -ūs *m.*	recess, distance back
reclūdō reclūdere reclūsī reclūsum	open up
recordor -ārī	remember
rēctŏr rēctōris *m.*	ruler
*rēctus -a -um *adj.*	straight; 209: facing ahead

*reddō reddere reddidī redditum	return, give back
*referō referre rettulī relātum	bring back, reply
refluō refluere	flow back, settle back
rēgia -ae *f.*	palace
*rēgnum -ī *n.*	kingdom
*relinquō relinquere relīquī relictum *tr.*	leave
rēmigium -ī *n.*	rowing
rēmus -ī *m.*	oar
*repente *adv.*	suddenly
*repōnō repōnere reposuī repositum	put back, put down
*rēs reī *f.*	thing, matter, property; 'reality'
reserō reserāre reserāvī reserātum	unlock
reservō reservāre reservāvī reservātum	keep back
resīdō resīdere resēdī resesssum	sit back down
revellō revellere revellī/vulsī revulsum	tear down
*rēx rēgis *m.*	king
*rīpa -ae *f.*	river-bank
rōbur rōboris *n.*	oak
*rogō rogāre rogāvī rogātum	ask (for), request
Rōmānus -a -um	Roman
rudō rudere rudīvī	bellow
ruīna -ae *f.*	destruction
rūmŏr rūmōris *m.*	sound

*rumpō rumpere rūpī ruptum	break, interrupt, disturb
rūpēs rūpis *f.*	cliff
sacer sacra sacrum *adj.*	sacred; **sacrum -ī** *n. as noun* ritual
*sacerdōs sacerdōtis *m. or f.*	priest(ess)
saeta -ae *f.*	bristle
*saevus -a -um *adj.*	dreadful
sagitta -ae *f.*	arrow
Salamis *acc.* **Salamīna**	Salamis, island ruled by Telamon, husband of Hesione
saltus -ūs *m.*	jump
sānctus -a -um *adj.*	sacred, holy
*sanguis sanguinis *m.*	blood
saturō saturāre saturāvī saturātum	fill, satiate
saxeus -a -um *adj.*	rocky
saxum -ī *n.*	rock
scelus sceleris *n.*	crime, wickedness
scindō scindere scidī scissum	divide
scopulus -ī *m.*	crag
*scūtum -ī *n.*	shield
scyphus -ī *m.*	*a type of large cup*
*sē (*or* **sēsē**) **suī sibi** (*or* **sibī**) **sē** *pron.*	him/her/itself, themselves
secō secāre secuī sectum	
*secundus -a -um *adj.*	supporting, favourable
secus *adv.*	otherwise (243: **non secus ac:** not otherwise than, i.e. 'just like')
*sed *conj.*	but
*sēdēs sēdis *f.*	place, home

sedīle sedīlis *n.*	seat
sēmifer -a -um *adj.*	half wild beast
sēmihomo sēmihominis *m.*	half-human
*semper *adv.*	always
*senātus -ūs *m.*	senate
sērus -a -um *adj.*	late
*servō servāre servāvī servātum	save, rescue, keep up
*sī *conj.*	if, if only (560)
*sīc *adv.*	thus
siccus -a -um	dry
sīdus sīderis *n.*	star, constellation
*signum -ī *n.*	sign, indication
silex silicis *f.*	rock
*silva -ae *f.*	wood
*simul *adv.*	at the same time
sīn *conj.*	but if
*socius -a -um *adj.*	allied, or as noun 'ally', 'friend'
*sōl sōlis *m.*	sun
solium -ī *n.*	throne, chair
sollemnis sollemne *adj.*	proper, solemn, 'due'
*sōlus -a -um *gen.* sōlius *adj.*	only, alone
*solvō solvere solvī solūtum	loosen, detach
*soror sorōris *f.*	sister
*spectō spectāre spectāvī spectātum	examine, try out
specus -ūs *m.*	cave
spēlunca -ae *f.*	cave
*spēs speī *f.*	hope, outlook
*spolia -ōrum *n.pl.*	spoils (of victory)
stabula -ōrum *n.pl.*	stopping-place
stāgnum -ī *n.*	still water, pool, lake

*statuō statuere statuī statūtum	establish
sternō sternere strāvī strātum *tr.*	spread out, lay down, lay low
stirps stirpis *f.*	stock, root
*stō stāre stetī statum	stand
strāvit *see* sternō	
*sub *prep.*+ *acc. & abl.*	under; + *acc.* down to
*subeō subīre subiī subitum	come into
subigō subigere subēgī subāctum	compel
*subitus -a -um *adj.*	sudden, unexpected
*sublātus *see* tollō	
subsistō subsistere substitī	pause, stop short
succēdō succēdere successī successum	come in to
*sum esse fuī	I am, to be *etc*
summoveō summovēre summōvī summōtum *tr.*	move away, move to a distance
super *prep. + acc. & abl.*	above; *adv.* (from) above; 251 = supererat 'remained'
superbus -a -um *adj.*	proud, arrogant
*superī -ōrum *m.pl.*	those above, the gods
*superō superāre superāvī superātum *tr. and intr.*	overcome, surpass
superstitiō -superstitiōnis *f.*	superstition
supplex supplicis *m. or f.*	suppliant
suprā *adv.*	above
suprēmus -a -um *adj.*	last
suspendō suspendere suspendī suspēnsum	hang; build as a vault (190)
sustineō sustinēre sustinuī	hold up, support

*suus -a -um adj.	his, her *etc.* ('belonging to the subject of the sentence/clause')
tābum -ī n.	putrefaction, decay
*tacitus -a -um adj.	quiet
*tālis tāle adj.	such
*tam adv.	so
*tamen conj.	nevertheless
*tantus -a -um adj.	so great
Tartarus -ī or Tartara n.pl.	Tartarus, the deepest pit of the Underworld
taurus -ī m.	bull
*tēctum -ī n.	roof, house
*tegō tegere tēxī tēctum	cover, shelter
*tēlum -ī n.	weapon, missile
temptāmentum -ī n.	experiment, trial
temptō temptāre temptāvī temptātum	attempt, make an attempt on
tendō -ere tetendī tentum/ tēnsum intr.	move, head (for)
tenebrae -ārum f.pl.	darkness
*teneō tenēre tenuī tentum	hold
tepeō tepēre	be warm
tepidus -a -um adj.	warm
ter adv.	three times
tergeminus -a -um adj.	triple
*tergum -ī n.	back
ternī -ae -a adj.	3 at a time, a set of 3
*terra -ae f.	earth, ground; *pl.* the world
*terreō terrēre terruī territum	terrify
terribilis terribile adj.	terrible
Teucrī -ōrum	another name for the Trojans

Thybris Thybridis	Tiber, the river or its god
***tibi** see **tū**	
***timeō timēre timuī**	fear
***timŏr timōris** *m.*	fear
Tīrynthius -a -um	'from Tiryns', epithet of Hercules (228)
***tollō tollere sustulī sublātum**	raise, remove
torreō torrēre torruī tostum	scorch, roast
torus -ī *m.*	cushion
***tot** *adv.*	so many
totidem *indecl. adj.*	the same number of times
***tōtus -a -um tōtius** *adj.*	whole
***trahō trahere traxī tractum**	drag
trepidō trepidāre trepidāvī trepidātum	panic
***trēs tria** *adj.*	three
***trīstis -e** *adj.*	grim, gloomy
***Troiānus -a -um** *adj.*	Trojan
Trōiŭgĕna -ae	Trojan
***tū tē (tuī) tibi** *or* **tibī tē**	you (*sing.*)
tueor -ērī tuitus/tūtus sum	gaze at
***tum** *adv.*	then ('at that time' or 'next')
tumeō tumēre tumuī	be swollen, run high
tumulus -ī *m.*	mound
tunc *adv.*	then, at that time
turbō turbāre turbāvī turbātum	confuse, upset
Turnus -ī	Turnus, leader of the Italians opposed to Aeneas
tūs tūris *m.*	incense
***tuus -a -um** *adj.*	your (*sing.*)

ubi conj. interrog:	where? *rel:* when, where
ullus -a -um ullius adj.	any
ultŏr ultōris *m.*	avenger
umbra -ae *f.*	shade
umbrōsus -a -um	shadowy
umerus -ī *m.*	shoulder
umquam adv.	ever
ūnā adv.	together with
ūnctus -a -um *adj., pp of* ūngō	waxed
*unda -ae *f.*	water, wave
unde adv.	where from? whence?
undique adv.	on all sides
*ūnus -a -um ūnĭus *or*	one
ūnīus *adj.*	
*urbs urbis *f.*	city
usquam *adv.*	anywhere
ut conj.	(1) (+ *subj.*) (i) so that (ii) *in indirect question* how (2) (+ *indic.*) as, when (3) *exclamatory adv.* how! (154)
vadum -ī *n.*	(shallow) water
vallis vallis *f.*	valley
vānus -a -um *adj.*	empty, useless
varius -a -um *adj.*	various, varied
vastus -a -um *adj.*	monstrous, desolate
vēlō vēlāre vēlāvī vēlātum	cover, shade
*veniō venīre vēnī ventum	come
*verbum -ī *n.*	word
verō adv.	indeed
vertex verticis *m.*	head, top
*vertō vertere vertī versum	turn, change

vescor vescī + *abl.*	feed on
*vester -tra -trum *adj.*	your ('of you' *pl.*)
vestīgium -ī *n.*	footprint, trace
vestiō vestīre vestīvī/vestiī vestītum	clothe, cover
*vetō vetāre vetuī vetitum	forbid
*vetus veteris *adj.*	old
*via -ae *f.*	way, route
*victŏr victōris *m.*	conqueror
*videō vidēre vīdī vīsum	see
viduō viduāre viduāvī viduātum	bereave
villōsus -a -um *adj.*	shaggy
vīnum -ī *n.*	wine
*vir virī *m.*	man; *gen. pl.* virum
viridis -e *adj.*	green
*virtūs virtūtis *f.*	courage, excellence
*vīs vim, -, vī, vīrēs, vīrium, vīribus *f.*	force
viscera viscerum *n.pl.*	flesh
vīsō vīsere vīsī	visit
vīsus -ūs *m.*	sight
*vīta -ae *f.*	life
vitta -ae *f.*	(ritual) woollen band
*vīvō vīvere vīxī vīctum	live
*vocō vocāre vocāvī vocātum	call (on)
Volcānus -ī	Vulcan, god of fire
*volō velle voluī	wish
volō volāre volāvī volātum	fly, move fast
volucris volucris *f.*	bird
voluptās voluptātis *f.*	pleasure, delight
vomō vomere vomuī vomitum	spew out

*vōs vōs (vestrum) vōbīs *pron*   you (*pl*)
*vōx vōcis *f.*   voice
*vulnerō vulnerāre vulnerāvī   wound
vulnerātum
*vultus -ūs *m.*   expression